D1164397

# FINDING YOUR

# NAVIGATING the COLLEGE ADMISSION PROCESS

KATRIN MUIR LAU
JUDITH WIDENER MUIR

**bright sky press**
HOUSTON, TEXAS

2015

*For Patti and Pat and all your family —*
*may you find*
*abundant joy in your journey*
*of discovery!*
*Jerry and Katrin*

**bright sky press**
HOUSTON, TEXAS

2365 Rice Blvd., Suite 202
Houston, Texas 77005

Copyright © 2015
No part of this book may be reproduced in any form or by any electronic or mechanical means, including information storage and retrieval devices or systems, without prior written permission from the publisher, except that brief passages may be quoted for reviews.

ISBN: 978-1-939055-xx-x

10   9   8   7   6   5   4   3   2   1

Library of Congress Cataloging-in-Publication Data on file with publisher.

Editorial Director, Lucy Chambers
Editor, Courtney Applewhite
Design, Marla Y. Garcia

Printed in Korea through Four Colour Print Group

# FINDING YOUR

# NAVIGATING the COLLEGE ADMISSION PROCESS

# ODE TO THE OFFICE OF ADMISSIONS

## OR
### *Wouldn't it be Nice to be Accepted by Rice*

A long while ago, so it seems,
I filled out your forms to the best of my means
Telling with answers most clear
Why I wanted to be an Owl Engineer.
    You see, I thought it would be nice
    To be accepted by Rice.

Then along came November
(How well I remember)
You said it must be understood
While I looked pretty good
That now I must wait
For an April date
    To find out if it was nice
    To be accepted by Rice

So I took more tests
To put me up among the rest
And sat back to wait
To see how I would rate.
Then along came April Ten
Only to be "Wait Listed" again.
    I find it's not so nice
    To be turned down twice.

So here I sit
Thinking, "Well kiss mah grits."
    (If you're wondering how that belongs in this refrain
    Remember, both Rice and grits are food—one a grass, one a
    grain)
But, what's that you say?
Come June, perhaps May,
There's a chance most thin
That I'll still get in.
    And finally hear you say, "It's nice
    To accept you at Rice."

P.S.
    So, Mr. Stabell
    Only time will tell
    But, I hope this brings a smile to some face
    At your most serious Acceptance place.
    One thing more let me say
    'Ere I fade quietly away:
    Think how much better this verse-would-be
    If I had training at Rice Uni-vers-ity.

– W.M.B.

Reproduced with permission from Richard M. Stabell
Dean of Admission Emeritus
Rice University

**WHAT LIES BEHIND YOU AND WHAT LIES IN FRONT OF YOU, PALES IN COMPARISON TO WHAT LIES INSIDE OF YOU.**

*– Ralph Waldo Emerson –*

# CONTENTS

# FINDING
## YOUR
## U

The college process can be perplexing, frustrating, and exhausting. We'd like to show you that it can also be liberating.

When you focus on who you are before turning your attention to what colleges have to offer, you can use the admission process to help you become the person you want to be.

It's a multi-step journey, and—as on any lengthy trek—a guide can help. We have helped hundreds of students navigate their way and secure admission to the college that's right for them. Now, we'd like to share what we know about the process with you.

The information explosion and technology transformation have changed everything—including the college application process. The electronic application makes it easier for more students to apply to more colleges, exponentially increasing the number of applicants. Escalating student debt is leading applicants to consider online courses, which are opening educational options not previously available. Issues are complex. Confusion is rampant. Emotions are volatile. All combine as a clarion call for good counseling.

While we can't promise you admission to a specific college, we can provide you with the best chance of gaining it. And as a mother and daughter who have been through this process together—both personally and professionally—we can provide you with tools to navigate the college application process from whatever point you begin your college journey.

# A MESSAGE
## ABOUT OUR
# PURPOSE

## TEAMWORK

If you are close enough to the college admission process to pick up this book, you are aware that the process is lengthy and complicated. You may be a high school student who has just had an introductory meeting with your school's counselor. You may be a parent who has just received a list of milestones for future paperwork and payments. Or you may be a college counselor who has gotten frustrated with the amount of time it takes to explain the process when what you really want to do is focus on your individual students. It is our firm belief that any process this long and multifaceted benefits from teamwork, so we have created this handbook to help all of us.

As college counselors who happen to be a mother and daughter, we have a unique perspective on the admission process. *Finding Your U* is the synthesis of our thirty years of work in this field, hundreds of college campus visits, and innumerable conversations with college deans and reps. Not only do we understand the nuances of what has become an increasingly complex process, but we also know that when students and parents can communicate with the correct information, the path to college applications can be a time of positive growth in both the student's self-awareness and the family's relationships.

We began by consolidating our accumulated files and notes; then we checked our practices and procedures against empirical research focusing on teen brain development. We have presented what we experience every day as counselors to you in a way that is more succinct and accessible than the current encyclopedic college counseling guides. We hope that this information will provide a useful handbook for domestic and international parents and students who are approaching American higher education with confusion or angst.

We have a remarkable collection of smart and savvy colleagues in the college counseling arena. Collectively, we have developed an expertise in sharing observations about our students as well as a large body of materials to serve our students and their families. But as much as we have learned about college admission, the process is rapidly changing. In *Finding Your U*, we have combined the most relevant traditional practices and information with the most up-to-date aspects of college admission. Much of what has been done until now simply does not make sense in the current digital landscape.

Whether you are a college applicant, a parent, or one of our counseling colleagues, we hope that having all this information in one easy-to-access place will provide more time for giving or receiving the personal counseling that is so important for making the best decisions in a complex world.

## WE NEED MORE TIME FOR COUNSELING

Why does it seem so difficult to get into college these days? There are several important factors: the increasing competition to gain a seat in the most selective colleges, the escalation of student debt, and the infusion of online educational opportunities all challenge families to rethink pathways to success. Despite these new challenges, the global marketplace will continue to reward the advanced training that colleges and universities provide because it positions students to take their seats at the global table and become the creative thinkers that the world needs.

As colleges seek to meet their own institutional needs in the face of volatile budgets, their process for admitting students has become less transparent and, therefore, more confusing. Their time and funds are increasingly limited. It is important to understand that the admission process itself is manageable and to approach it efficiently and with clear intention. We have seen many students and families so caught up in the details or the competition of the application process that they failed to look thoughtfully at where to apply and why.

## WE CHANGED THE QUESTIONS
## IN ORDER TO GET BETTER ANSWERS.

We analyzed the way we engage college-bound teens—the questions we ask, the lists we provide, and the resources we suggest. We sought to take out the guilt and the fear and to minimize the stress and anxiety. The stress response system kicks in when we feel out of control—and that feeling is the hallmark of the college application process.

The parents we work with are as emotional as their teens: they cannot control outcome; they are about to lose a child from their nest; and they anticipate having to spend a fortune trying to position their child to have career stability and social mobility. Families come to us torn apart with conflicting emotions.

Our role is to help you and your family to navigate the process, define success, and move forward in the best way possible. Our experience and understanding of the process can help you approach it as rationally as possible.

In reviewing our materials, we have discovered that the adjectives and prompts many of us have been using to jump-start personal reflection and college research may not consistently resonate with teens: do you want big or small, public or private, urban or rural. A high school student often has no experiential base as a reference to know the answers to those kinds of questions. So we changed the questions to get better answers: what do you feel deeply about, do you want to be close to home, need an airport close by, like to know your professors personally, want people surrounding you who are like you. When you can relate to the question and answer in meaningful ways, the questions can lead you to discovering who you are becoming, what you value, and where you can learn best.

Self-discovery: the college application process needs to start there. Getting to know ourselves is a luxury that we seldom allow or take time to indulge in. But before making any good fit in our lives, we need to know a great deal about who we are. Whether we are choosing a life partner, a career, or buying a house, the question of fit calls out. It matters. Fitting in to tomorrow's choices demands that today's questions be more relevant. Finding your college or university requires that you first find your "you." Without that understanding, the scope of choices is overwhelming and finding the best fit is more difficult.

## THE PAST MEETS THE PRESENT

As we worked side by side as mother and daughter, we found we were personally experiencing the transition in communication styles and formats. We laughed at ourselves as we captured the generational differences in language, format, and even expectations. We discovered that together we had a remarkably useful amalgam of experience, and that revelation was thrilling. Our approach became mother conveying tried-and-true wisdom to daughter, with daughter freshening it up, keeping the best of the past and enriching it with the present. We have both seen first-hand that doing everything the same old way does not serve today's students. Yet by hopping on the digital train too quickly and too completely, some deeply important ideas and practices that have anchored generations past can become lost.

So, here we acknowledge the brilliance of those who have come before us, those who have stood with us, and those with whom we seek to understand the future. Thank you to the multitude of colleagues with whom we have worked, learned, and celebrated over the years! And thank you to the students whom we all serve, for reminding us that we must learn from you as much as we teach you. By sharing the best of what we know, and encouraging you to communicate with the team that is in place to help you navigate the path to college, it is our hope that you will truly find your "U."

# WHY
## AMERICAN HIGHER
# EDUCATION
## IS UNIQUE

### WHAT'S THE DIFFERENCE BETWEEN A COLLEGE AND A UNIVERSITY?

E very aspect of the college admission process seems to raise more questions. The first thing many people wonder is what's the difference between a college and a university? Although the words "college" and "university" are often used interchangeably, they actually were formed for different purposes.

- A college "transmits knowledge of and from the past in their liberal arts programs to undergraduate students so they may draw upon it as a living resource in the future."
- A university comprises faculty and graduate students "with the aim of creating new knowledge in order to supersede the past."
- Colleges may exist as divisions of a university.

As with many beliefs surrounding higher education in America, generalizations and stereotypes abound. The general impression of colleges is that they are smaller and more personalized—with a focus on teaching, rather than research—and that they are more expensive as a result. By contrast, universities are generally larger and the perception is that their professors engage more in research than in teaching undergraduates. Yet opportunities can exist for young scholars to work with professors in cutting-edge research in both a college and a university. Both colleges and universities can be places of deep learning, and their educational differences have become more and more blurry over the decades. For purposes of this book, we will use the word college interchangeably for either a college or a university experience.

## THE PURSUIT OF SELF-KNOWLEDGE

College has, historically, been the place that Americans send their adolescents in pursuit of self-knowledge. It's a place where you can reflect on the best thoughts and ideas of the past in order to better understand the future challenges that await you; a place where humanities and sciences and arts co-exist; a place where nascent scholars learn to respect perspectives beyond their own; a place where relationships grow that can ignite your mind and spirit. In arguing the advantages of a liberal arts education where students dip into multiple disciplines, Kingman Brewster, an outspoken former president of Yale, said, "Perhaps the most fundamental value of a liberal arts education is that it makes life more interesting. It also makes it less likely that you will be bored with life—or that you, in turn, will be boring to your colleagues and friends."

## TIME FOR PERSONAL DISCOVERY

A fundamental difference between American higher education and that in Europe and other international communities is the student mindset when they arrive. In Europe, a student selects a field of study in advance and does not waver from this discipline. In America, you can defer that selection for up to the first two years of formal study, an opportunity that provides you time to discover the area of aptitude and interest that may be the best fit for future productivity. This delay in decision-making provides students in American colleges time to figure out who they are and live their lives in a way that is right for them and responsible to the community.

## WHAT SHOULD YOU LEARN IN COLLEGE?

Currently there is widespread debate over what you should be learning during your college years and what you'll need to know when you complete your degree program. The information explosion and transformative technology have spurred arguments about the best way to prepare you for the world you will enter. Economic instability and globalization are causing college presidents to rethink their mission. Online learning is rapidly expanding, challenging the classroom lecture that has dominated formal education for the past 600 years. William Bowen, a former Princeton president, notes "these technologies have already proven their value for fields where there is 'a single right answer' to many questions." Yet the British scholar, Alison Wolf, disagrees in saying "we have not found any low-cost, high technology alternatives to expert human teachers—at least not yet."

## THE CALL FOR APPROPRIATE FIT

So, what's the best option for you? American higher education boasts over 3,000 institutions, offering a smorgasbord that is at once exciting and overwhelming: urban and rural, large and small, public and private, religious and secular. Some are highly selective; some admit almost all who apply. American higher education is teeming with choice, but finding an appropriate fit between you and your eventual college remains a top priority. The challenge for families and counselors in the application process is to guide you in navigating the journey of self-discovery and understanding the nuances of the many programs in order to create the educational fit that propels personal growth. The challenge for *you* is to work with *them* with an open mind and cooperative spirit. A good college experience can be transformative.

## CHOICE IS THE STRENGTH OF AMERICAN HIGHER EDUCATION

American higher education can be confusing. We want to help you understand why choice is its strength and how the admission process is, at its core, reasonable and manageable. We have broken down the process into workable units to help you understand your options, navigate the required documents, and tell your stories in a poignant way to help admission deans understand the ways in which you can enrich a college community so you may gain admission to the institution of higher learning that is your personal best fit.

# HOW
## YOU DECIDE
# WHERE
## TO APPLY

## THE PROCESS

The college application process is an increasingly complex and expensive system. As in any system, you will encounter jargon, trends, procedures, and choices. The time you spend in this process will go more smoothly if you have some help translating the lingo, targeting the hot topics, unraveling the protocol, and personalizing the options. That's where we fit in.

A successful college search will result in a positive fit between you and an institution, and that fit that will maximize your personal growth and productivity. By combining introspection with active investigation, you will ultimately be able to make informed decisions based on fact rather than superficial perception. Your self-assessment and college investigation will help you develop a strong sense of personal direction that will enable you to take ownership of the college application process.

Before you attempt to decide where you will apply, you should start with a process of self-discovery. Investigating colleges requires identifying some of your own needs first.

Take a moment to write down some thoughts you may have had about what you are looking for in a college:

_____

_____

_____

_____

_____

_____

_____

_____

_____

_____

_____

_____

_____

_____

_____

_____

_____

_____

_____

_____

_____

> Fit is intangible. It is very personal.
> It will feel right. It may wrap around the
> environment, facilities, professors, or students.
> You will know when you have found it.

## FINDING YOUR FIT
### Finding Your U Begins with You!

Be thoughtful as you answer these questions—patterns will emerge that can jump-start your college search to help you find your best college fit.

| LOCATION | Y | N | ? |
|---|---|---|---|
| I need to be close to home. | | | |
| I need to be close to a major airport. | | | |
| I would feel trapped if not in close proximity to a city. | | | |
| I need to be in an environment where I can explore my interests off campus. | | | |
| The physical beauty of my environment is very important to me. | | | |
| The climate where the school is located is an important factor. | | | |

| ACADEMICS | Y | N | ? |
|---|---|---|---|
| I want to know my professors and have them available to me. | | | |
| I learn best in small classes. | | | |
| There are specific facilities I will need for my area of study—laboratories, studio space, or equipment. | | | |
| I would like to experiment widely in the curriculum and change majors easily if I choose. | | | |
| I need a structured curriculum with clearly defined core requirements, requirements in my designated major, and optional electives. | | | |
| I need a challenging academic environment where most of the students are at my ability level or higher. | | | |

| STUDENT BODY | Y | N | ? |
|---|---|---|---|
| I want to know most of the people I go to school with. | | | |
| I want these people to be like me—same religious background, part of the country, or values. | | | |
| I want anonymity on campus. | | | |

| CAMPUS LIFE | Y | N | ? |
|---|---|---|---|
| I want to live on campus. | | | |
| I would like to belong to a fraternity or sorority. | | | |
| I want strong school spirit where most students go to athletic events. | | | |
| I would like to participate in college athletics. | | | |
| Division I | | | |
| Division II | | | |
| Division III | | | |
| Club Level | | | |
| Intramural | | | |
| I want to participate in specific extracurricular activities. | | | |
| Theater | | | |
| Music | | | |
| Service | | | |
| Specific Club | | | |
| Other | | | |

# LEARNING ABOUT COLLEGES

## Getting on Campus

Now that you have identified your priorities, it's time to learn about the colleges. Your first goal is to get to a college campus, even if it is not necessarily a school that you are seriously thinking of attending. Start local. You need to feel the difference between a large public university and a small liberal arts college. Drive to your state university. Stop along the way to explore any other campuses in the area. If you really cannot get to any college campus, look online at virtual tours.

## Informational Resources

The best source of accurate details about a college will be its own website, but guidebooks and general websites can be a helpful place to start your research. Some guidebooks—like the *College Board College Handbook*—are objective: they will provide comprehensive information with factual information about majors, athletics, programs on campus, and statistical data. On the other hand, subjective guidebooks—like the *Fiske Guide to Colleges*—are interpretive, combining facts and opinions to give you a sense of the campus culture. You can also talk directly to current students through social media. You will learn more about these guides later in this chapter.

Colleges buy mailing lists from the standardized testing services based on their institutional priorities. You can learn a great deal from the material you will be inundated with as soon as your test scores are released. Be open-minded; you might discover a new college or program. If you have any interest in a college that reaches out to you, be sure to respond. Demonstrated interest can become a significant factor in the decision to admit a student.

## Search Engines

While you continue to search college websites as your primary source of accurate information, remember to look both broadly and specifically. You can search by major fields of study, religious affiliation, geographic regions, sports programs, size, and cost. As you search, be aware that different areas of study might be placed in different departments at a college. For instance, marketing is sometimes a business major and sometimes a communications major. College Board provides a useful search engine at *www.collegeboard.com.*

## Rankings

Beware of being swayed by rankings. Consumers often gravitate to them looking for quick answers. Don't choose your college based on its rank. A ranking is not necessarily an assessment of a best fit for you. Rankings can also be manipulated. While rankings may be a place to start, they will not likely provide the ultimate information you need to determine your personal fit.

## Selectivity

Most students apply to about a dozen schools. Have a range of selectivity on your list as you narrow it down: highly selective, moderately selective, and probable based on your personal profile and what you have learned about each college. Remember that admission decisions take into account more factors than merely grades and test scores. Avoid getting emotionally attached to one "dream" school; there is more than one place where you can find happiness and be productive. Even if you have a "perfect profile," admission decisions can still be a wild card because institutional priorities can vary from season to season.

> There are many ways to research the differences among the colleges and universities. Stay focused on what is important to you.

# CONTACTING COLLEGES

## College Representatives

If you are interested in a certain college, getting to know a representative from there is valuable both to you and to the representative. The representative is your personal contact with an otherwise faceless institution, a person to whom you can turn with questions or concerns and who will give you personal attention. The representative may also be directly involved in the review of your application, so it's helpful to the representative to know who you are when he reads your file. Additionally, your contact with the representative demonstrates your seriousness about attending that college, which provides you an advantage in the application review process. There are several ways to establish contact with college representatives.

## Information Sessions

Many colleges offer local evening or weekend information sessions once or twice a year in a facility such as a hotel ballroom or conference center. The purpose of these sessions is to give you, as a potential applicant, an in-depth look at the college—including its admission policies, academic programs, graduation requirements, extracurricular activities, and financial assistance programs. The presenters are usually members of the admission staff, so this is a good opportunity to begin to develop rapport with a staff member. Be sure to sign the attendance log and dress appropriately.

## College Fairs

College Fairs are held in many cities during the fall semester, often in high school gymnasiums. At college fairs, college representatives sit behind tables laden with brochures and other informational pieces so you can stop by to pick up materials or ask questions. The representative may be a member of the college's admission staff or an alumni representative. College Fairs provide excellent opportunities to gather college materials and to learn about colleges that you know little about. Pre-register so the college representative can scan the barcode on your nametag to get your information, saving time and ensuring accurate contact information.

## School Visits

During the fall semester, admission officers visit high schools around the country to meet with prospective applicants. These sessions are extremely valuable because they are typically your first opportunity to spend extended time with a representative from that college in the absence of a large crowd. They provide a prime opportunity both for gathering information and for making a good impression. Come to the sessions with questions in mind, a positive attitude, and a neat appearance. Be polite and respectful to the admissions representative and to your peers. This person will likely be the first admissions officer to read your application, should you choose to apply to that college.

## Via Email

Representatives welcome emails from prospective students, as long as the messages ask questions that cannot be answered by reading the school's website or brochures. Be respectful of their time, and remember to use traditional punctuation and spelling, rather than what might be appropriate for social media sites. The impression your email makes is important, too.

# CAMPUS VISITS

An ideal way for you to assess a college is the campus visit. College websites provide the hard data about their programs, facilities, and what it takes to gain admission. Being on a college campus helps you decide if you can see yourself there. You'll get a sense of the space, the proximity of dorms to classrooms, and the energy level of the students: are they friendly, are they competitive, how rigorous is their academic load? Many colleges offer virtual tours, as well; in addition, there are websites dedicated to virtual tours beyond those the colleges provide themselves. Be aware that to promote their programs colleges will offer fly-ins, all expenses covered by the college, for their top recruits. Whether you are invited or you go on your own as most students do, plan ahead, go with anticipation, and leave with the information you need to make a decision based on fact rather than hype.

## Before you visit

Schedule an appointment for an official campus tour, via phone or website.

Register for an information session.

If appropriate because of your special interests or demonstrated talents, make arrangements to meet with a faculty member or a coach to identify if a specific program is a potential fit for you.

If you are ready to sit in on classes or even spend a night in a residence hall, ask the admission office to help you facilitate the arrangements. Many colleges have specific weekends scheduled for prospective student visits.

## While you're on campus

### Find Students

Ask them what they like about their college and what has disappointed them.

Inquire about faculty accessibility, academic workloads, and social life.

Ask what they do on the weekend. Are they on campus or off campus? Does the college organize activities? Is there a large fraternity and sorority scene? Will you need a car?

Take note of the general student body. Do students seem happy? Are they respectful of one another? What's the diversity level? How do students socialize? Does their general intellectual level seem similar to your own?

### Investigate Housing

What are the housing options for freshmen?

Will you have guaranteed housing all four years?

What furniture is included in student housing?

How clean are the common areas?

### Check out the Dining Facilities

What are the options for meal plans? Make sure to sample the food.

Look to see what dining options exist beyond the campus.

Will your meal plan cover meals in any off-campus restaurants? Ask how frequently students eat out.

### Notice the Campus Atmosphere

Is it urban, rural; large, small; public, private?

Ask for campus security statistics. Is there a shuttle to take you home at night?

Get a school newspaper and explore the current issues. What are students complaining about? How does the administration deal with controversy?

Read posted flyers on kiosks to get ideas about available activities and to see how students use their time outside of class.

Check out the bookstore and student center.

*Specialty Programs*

Investigate academic departments and specialty programs you want to pursue, and consider structuring your time to attend specific events. Take time to visit:

- ⊙ Athletic facilities
- ⊙ Fine arts programs
- ⊙ Research labs
- ⊙ Intramural programs
- ⊙ Journalism opportunities
- ⊙ Career placement services
- ⊙ Academic support
- ⊙ Libraries

*Follow-up*

Jot down your impressions immediately. Take pictures.

Details of campus visits will begin to blur and what you recall may become more difficult to substantiate; your impression will take on renewed importance as you visit multiple colleges and try to sort through your reason for choosing one over the others. Create your own spreadsheet that covers what is important to you.

Follow your instincts, but base them on solid research and a cross-section of observations among yourself, your family, and your friends. Your job is to ferret out the places where you can find an intellectual and social fit, a place where you will be challenged and will be happy for four years.

**Remember:** There is more than one college where you can find happiness and become a productive citizen!

## SUMMERS

Summer offers an opportunity for intellectual growth, artistic achievement, personal service, and adventure. A summer experience can help you identify an unexplored talent—one that you can nurture over time and that can become a distinguisher in the college admission process.

Being away from home can be a catalyst for personal growth. Functioning among your peers from other regions and countries can be instructional, as well. Many summer programs manage to combine academic pursuits with the traditional joys of summer.

A summer job or internship can help you identify areas for your future study and professional direction. Building relationships remains a focal point in learning about topics and about yourself.

Many boarding schools offer multiple and varied classes in combination with strong sports and recreational options.

Colleges offer high school students intensive coursework, as well as cultural and enrichment opportunities. These programs offer an excellent opportunity for students to experience different geographic locations and types of college environments. Some college programs provide their own professors; some feature programs that rent the college spaces and bring in their own teams.

Programs abroad, academic or language intensive, provide strong opportunities for cultural growth.

Sports clinics, art training, and subject-specific programs—such as architecture, space camp, or hot topics like entrepreneurship or global studies—enable a student to investigate areas of special interest, developing excellence in a specific area.

Adventure carries its own quiet lessons about self-confidence and personal potential.

Volunteer work can be enriching and may have the added advantage of a flexible schedule. Match your interests and skills.

Use programs as a starting point for thinking about possibilities. Sometimes the theme can inspire you to create your own experience. Peruse websites by topic, program type, college, geography, museum, or boarding school to begin your search and jump-start your personal self-discovery.

> The summer experience does not have to be expensive or spectacular, it should simply be personally appropriate.

### Seize the Summer!
Summer provides an ideal time for intellectual growth, achievement, and adventure.

- Develop artistic or athletic talents
- Investigate a new academic area
- Explore a new geographic region
- Attend specialty training programs
- Seek meaningful internships
- Volunteer
- Study abroad

# INTERNSHIPS

Learning happens best in meaningful relationships with mentors who make lessons relevant and interactive—the hallmarks of a successful internship. An internship can last a day, a week, a summer, or a semester—whatever time frame works for you and for your sponsor. Some internships might be project or research-based; some might have to be "job shadowing" to appease the parameters of Human Resource Departments and to comply with federal mandates about not exploiting minors.

Strategic planning for appropriate internships requires that you scrutinize your interests and aptitudes. Internships provide a vehicle for learning about the global marketplace you will enter, building a network in the business community, thinking about potential college majors and future career paths, securing an additional letter of recommendation from someone who will know you in a different context, and—most important—learning about yourself. Experience shapes your journey. Experience crafts your story. Experience molds you and unleashes your potential.

Pulling out a ready-made list of internship options and then matching names of hopeful interns to it can easily miss the target. The match of intern and mentor defines the depth of your learning and the impact the experience will have on your future. It is the understanding that you gain and the story you can tell about the work you did—not the name of the organization on a neon sign—that will capture the attention of the admission officer who is lucky enough to read your well-crafted resume where you quantify the details of your experience and contribution.

Internships invite you to interact with your world. Be appropriately aggressive and sleuth out the opportunities that await you. Create your own experiences. Using initiative to find a good internship is a growth experience in itself. Push out the walls of your classrooms and stretch your learning.

# DEGREES: OPTIONS TO PURSUE

While most students obtain their degrees on a college campus, online options also exist and offer the advantage of flexible scheduling and lower cost. The following is an overview of the most common college degrees, what they require, and what students can expect from the experience.

| DEGREE | EXAMPLES | |
|---|---|---|
| **Associate Degree**<br>The associate's degree can allow a student to enter the work force directly upon graduation, or it can be a stepping-stone to a bachelor's degree. Programs vary from one to three years. Degrees are frequently granted by junior colleges, community colleges, or online organizations. A high school diploma is required before entering these programs. | Associate of Arts<br>Associate of Science | **A.A.**<br>**A.S.** |
| **Bachelor's Degree**<br>The most often earned college degree, a bachelor's degree is generally offered as a liberal arts, science, professional, or pre-professional program and normally obtained in four years. Many entry-level jobs require a bachelor's degree. | Bachelor of Arts<br>Bachelor of Fine Arts<br>Bachelor of Science<br>Bachelor of Business<br>Administration<br>Bachelor of Music<br>Bachelor of<br>Architecture<br>Bachelor of Science<br>in Nursing | **B.A.**<br>**B.F.A.**<br>**B.S.**<br><br>**B.B.A.**<br>**B.M.**<br><br>**B.Arch.**<br><br>**B.S.N.** |
| In some instances, the bachelor's degree is the first step towards higher educational attainment—for instance, fields like law and medicine require additional training. | | |

| DEGREE | EXAMPLES |
|---|---|
| **Certification** <br> Certificate programs can provide additional specialty training when a working professional needs to become certified in a new technology, or needs to fulfill a requirement for entry into a particular field. Both state and professional organizations frequently require a certificate before a person is allowed legally to do certain kinds of work. Many certificate programs are available online. | Emergency Medical Technician   **E.M.T.** <br> Certified Public Accountant   **C.P.A.** <br> Certified Engineering Technician   **C.E.A.** <br> Physician Assistant   **P.A.-C.** |
| **Master's Degree** <br> The first graduate degree earned in the liberal arts, sciences, and certain professional fields, a master's degree usually takes one to two years of full-time study. Entry into a master's degree program, whether on a campus or online, usually requires completion of a bachelor's degree and the attainment of certain scores on a graduate level exam such as the GRE or GMAT. Many students who enter online master's degree programs have already entered the workforce and are trying to earn a higher degree for a promotion or salary boost. Online degree programs can allow these students to work on courses at a time that is convenient for them, so they can earn their degree within the framework of their work or family commitments. | Masters of Arts   **M.A.** <br> Masters of Fine Arts   **M.F.A.** <br> Master of Arts in Teaching   **M.A.T.** <br> Master of Science   **M.S.** <br> Master of Education   **M.Ed.** <br> Master of Business Administration   **M.B.A.** <br> Master of Healthcare Administration   **M.H.A.** <br> Master of Computer Science   **M.C.S.** <br> Master of Architecture   **M. Arch.** <br> Master of Liberal Arts   **M.L.A.** <br> Master of Divinity   **M.Div.** <br> Master of Fine Arts   **M.F.A.** <br> Master of Social Work   **M.S.W.** <br> Master of Library Science   **M.L.S.** <br> Master of Public Administration   **M.P.A.** <br> Master of Public Policy   **M.P.P.** |

| DEGREE | EXAMPLES |
|---|---|
| **Doctorate** <br> The highest degree awarded in research-oriented academic disciplines, earning a doctorate usually requires from three to six additional years of full-time study. | Doctor of Dental Science    **D.D.S.** <br> Doctor of Education    **Ed.D.** <br> Doctor of Veterinary Medicine    **D.V.M.** <br> Doctor of Jurisprudence    **J.D.** <br> Doctor of Psychology    **Psy.D.** <br> Doctor of Philosophy (almost any subject)    **Ph.D.** <br> Medical Doctor    **M.D.** <br> Doctor of Pharmacy    **Pharm.D.** |

# SOURCE BOOKS

### The Big Ones: Objective Guides

These enormous reference books contain the most up-to-date statistics about colleges and universities. These books are great resources for finding out basic information about specific colleges of interest to you, as well as for looking up colleges according to certain criteria, such as geographical area or majors offered.

⊙ *Profiles of American Colleges.* Barron's Educational Series
⊙ *Four-Year Colleges.* Peterson's Guides
⊙ *College Handbook.* The College Board

### The Fun Ones: Subjective Guides

These guides provide less raw data and more description. They discuss aspects of colleges such as campus culture and the most popular majors. Subjective in nature, these books nicely complement the more objective reference guides mentioned above.

⊙ *The Fiske Guide to Colleges* by Edward Fiske. Written by the former education editor of *The New York Times*, this guide offers in-depth analysis of each college's academic strengths and many other interesting details.
⊙ *College Match: A Blueprint for Choosing the Best School for You* by Steven Antonoff. A combination of easy-to-use worksheets and loads of practical advice to guide students through the college process.
⊙ *Colleges That Change Lives: 40 Schools That Will Change the Way You Think About Colleges* by Loren Pope and Hilary Masell Oswald. Profiles of great schools for students who are looking for a good fit, not just the college with the most competitive admission or famous name.
⊙ *Looking Beyond the Ivy League: Finding the College That's Right for You* by Loren Pope. An authoritative, carefully expressed argument for aiming at a small liberal-arts college rather than a large, impersonal university. Pope claims that there is "a lot of non-Ivy quality available" for many kinds of students, and describes several colleges and programs to back up his points.

## The Off-Beat One: Unique Perspectives

This book helps when you are looking for colleges with particular philosophies or unusual majors.

⊙ *Cool Colleges: For the Hyper-Intelligent, Self-Directed, Late Blooming, and Just Plain Different* by Donald Asher. A collection of iconoclastic schools across the country and what makes them stand out.

## The Personal Ones: The Emotional Impact of the Application Process

The college application process can be emotional for the whole family. These books contain practical advice on how to navigate the confusing and complex process.

⊙ *The College Admissions Mystique* by Bill Mayher. A practical and eye-opening view of the application and admission process from a former college counselor. This book is directed at both students and parents.

⊙ *Acceptance: A Legendary Guidance Counselor Helps Seven Kids Find the Right Colleges – and Find Themselves* by David Marcus. This book provides a glimpse into the college application process following a diverse group of seniors and shows how the dreams of the students meet the reality of the admissions process.

⊙ *The Gatekeepers: Inside the Admissions Process of a Premier College* by Jacques Steinberg. An in-depth look into the life of an admission officer at Wesleyan University, revealing the college admission process in behind-the-scene detail.

# USEFUL WEBSITES

## College Search Tools

⊙ *www.collegeboard.org*
Search engine and makers of the SAT and CSS Profile

⊙ *www.fairtest.org*
Site to find test-optional schools

⊙ *www.nacacnet.org*
National Association of College Admission Counselors

## College Applications and Resources

⊙ *www.commonapp.org*
An application site for many colleges

⊙ *www.universalcollegeapp.com*
An application site for many colleges

## Standardized Testing

⊙ *www.collegeboard.org*
Search engine and SAT information

⊙ *www.actstudent.org*
Information and scheduling for the ACT standardized test

⊙ *www.ets.org*
Information and scheduling for the TOEFL test

⊙ *www.ielts.org*
Information and scheduling for the IELTS test

## Collegiate Athletics

⊙ *www.ncaa.com*
National Collegiate Athletic Association Clearinghouse.
Site with up-to-date information and regulations for college athletes

⊙ *www.eligibilitycenter.org*
Site where all college athletes need to register

## Financial Aid

- *www.ed.gov*
  The Department of Education Website for financial information
- www.fafsa.ed.gov
  Site to register for government financial aid
- www.collegeboard.org
  Site to complete an institutional profile
- www.studentaid.ed.gov
  Government site with lists of useful links

> Individual college websites are the most up-to-date and comprehensive places to find specific information.

# HOW
## COLLEGES DECIDE
# WHO
## GETS IN

Colleges look closely at course selection, academic growth, and personal involvement in school and community life when they review their applicants. Therefore, working to your potential on coursework while identifying areas where personal initiative, leadership, and special talent might emerge should be your focus throughout high school. How do your efforts affect the colleges' decisions?

## THE PROCESS

Colleges are looking for evidence of a mind at work, intellectual curiosity, and personal initiative. Admission committees balance your academic record and personal profile. Each is important because a college is putting together a class that will contribute to the intellectual vigor and social energy of the school. The importance of each piece will vary with the selectivity and needs of the college.

*"HOLISTIC ADMISSION means reviewing academic excellence demonstrated by original writing and research, extracurricular activities, and community involvement. Personal qualities and character are also fundamental to every decision. The admissions committee seeks students whose backgrounds and life experiences will be educational for fellow classmates. Teacher recommendations, interviews, essays, and other qualitative information provided by applicants also help inform admissions decisions."*

    — **William Fitzsimmons**
    Dean of Admissions and Financial Aid
    Harvard College
    *Harvard Gazette 2013*

Admission officers will focus on the following categories as they seek to make a decision on your file:

## Academic Record

⊙ Transcript/course selection
  • Did you go beyond the requirements?
⊙ Grade Point Average
⊙ Class Position
⊙ Standardized test scores (some colleges are test optional)
  • For a list of standardized tests, see page 48

## Personal Profile

- Extracurricular activities
  - How did you spend your time outside of class?
- Leadership experiences
  - Where did you demonstrate initiative?
- Personal talents/special attributes
- Work experiences
- Volunteer experiences
- Summer experiences
  - Did you pursue specialty training to develop a talent or explore new academic, artistic, or athletic areas?

## The Application: Putting it all together

- Essays
- Resume
- Letters of Recommendation
- Interviews
- Demonstrated Interest

In all cases, the application itself carries immense importance. Well-presented details can lead an admission officer to see a mutually beneficial connection between you and the institution.

# STANDARDIZED TESTING

Once you enter high school, you begin to notice that test scores permeate the news and the conversations around you. Remember that scores are important, but they are only one part of your application. These scores do not define who you are; they do not measure creativity, determination, or emotional intelligence. The burning question is always, "What is a good score?" The absolute answer is always "It depends." Schools publish the range of their students' scores, but there are always outliers—those students who demonstrate special talents that the college needs to shape its community as a learning environment.

Colleges use the following standardized test scores (some colleges are test optional):

- ⊙ SAT test
- ⊙ SAT subject tests
- ⊙ ACT test
- ⊙ AP (Advanced Placement) tests
- ⊙ IB (International Baccalaureate) tests

## The SAT Test

The SAT test, originally named Scholastic Aptitude Test, is a reasoning test consisting of a reading section, a math section, a writing section, and an essay. The essay may or may not be optional beginning in 2016 depending on the college. Each section's highest score is 800 points. The essay receives a score ranging from 2 to 12. The purpose of this test is to convey important information about a student's strengths and needs through a series of scores.

Colleges can look at standardized test scores in several ways.
1. Look at every test taken
2. Look at scores from single test dates
3. Super Score – using the highest individual scores from different subtests to compile the highest composite score

4. Super Duper Score – using highest individual scores from different subtests of the SAT and ACT to compile the highest composite score

## The ACT Test

ACT, American College Testing, is a curriculum-based achievement test that provides an academic assessment of student ability. This test showcases mastery of classroom material. All colleges will accept the ACT as well as the SAT. Students need to try both to see which one is their better fit. The ACT has four multiple-choice tests—English, Math, Reading, Science Reasoning—each scored 1 to 36, then averaged together for a composite score. There is also an optional essay worth 2 to 12 points. Most colleges require the essay section. Colleges look at both section scores and composite scores. Some colleges are beginning to Super Score the ACT.

### A Word about the PSAT/NMSQT

The Preliminary Scholastic Aptitude Test/National Merit Scholarship Qualifying Test is administered by high schools during October of the junior year. To qualify as a National Merit Scholar, a student must hold United States citizenship and achieve a predetermined score that varies from state to state. The PSAT is a practice test for the SAT.

Of particular note: While PSAT scores do not appear on a college application, they are useful for the following:

⊙ Identifying academic sections you need to work on
⊙ Summer programs may request them
⊙ Colleges use the scores to target potential applicants
⊙ Qualifiers for honors and scholarships

Take sample SAT and ACT tests to decide which fits you best. As a consumer, you have a choice—it is to your advantage to try both.

## The SAT Subject Tests

These subject matter tests demonstrate mastery in specific academic areas. Check individual college websites for admission requirements. Not all colleges require these exams, but they can offer an opportunity to distinguish an applicant as a scholar in a specific content area. Some colleges will use these tests for college course placement. Generally, students take the SAT subject tests immediately following the high school course. The top score is 800. The following are examples of subject tests that the College Board may offer:

| | |
|---|---|
| Biology | Latin |
| Chemistry | Literature |
| Chinese with Listening | Math I & II |
| French | Modern Hebrew |
| French with Listening | Physics |
| German | Spanish |
| German with Listening | Spanish with Listening |
| Italian | U.S. History |
| Japanese with Listening | World History |
| Korean with Listening | |

## AP Exams

Advance Placement Exams are designed to come at the culmination of advanced placement high school classes in over 30 different subject areas. These tests are scored from 1 to 5, 5 being the highest. While some colleges may use these for admissions, most use them for course credit—check each college's website for details. AP tests can become a distinguisher to demonstrate mastery. Generally, students take the AP exams immediately following the high school course.

## IB Exams

The International Baccalaureate offers yet another way to demonstrate academic mastery to colleges. Historically, IB has been a measuring stick for schools outside the United States. A student can achieve either an IB Certificate or an IB Diploma. Many colleges award scholarships and college course credit for scores of 4 to 7, usually in higher-level courses. Most colleges have high regard for the IB Diploma. An IB Diploma can significantly impact a decision for admission. IB Predicted Grades can be sent throughout the school year, while final scores are sent in July following the senior year.

## Practice the Tests

Take practice tests! Being familiar with the test can increase your score. Practice pacing yourself for each section so you do not run out of time. Use diagnostic tests to review weak points to improve your skills. Familiarity with the test—knowing what to expect—can help minimize stress on the test day. Practice tests are readily available online and at bookstores.

> Begin building an appropriate standardized testing profile.

## Advice for Test Day

⊙ Plan your route to the test
⊙ Pack your backpack with essential items
- Admission ticket
- Photo Identification
- No. 2 pencils and eraser
- An acceptable calculator
- A jacket
- A wristwatch
⊙ Get a good night's sleep
⊙ Eat a hearty breakfast
⊙ Arrive early

> **Remember:** while test scores matter, you are more than a number.

# APPLICATIONS

Colleges offer you the option of regular decision, rolling decision, early action, single choice early action, and early decision. You should check individual college websites for policies and protocol unique to each college as their dates, regulations, and forms can change year to year. Colleges will give you different submission options: by their website, specific application websites, a state-specific website, or by mail.

Student applicants are responsible for the following:
⊙ Filling out applications
⊙ Checking each college deadline
⊙ Signing waiver, relinquishing right to read recommendations
⊙ Signing release form, giving college office permission to send transcripts and recommendations to your list of colleges
⊙ Sending standardized test scores to each college
⊙ Signing early decision agreement with intent to enroll, if applicable
⊙ Submitting applications

When submitting your application, make sure you have finished every section:
• Main application
• Supplements
• Application fee

High school college counselors provide the supporting documents, submitting for you:
⊙ Counselor letter of recommendation
⊙ Secondary School Report form
⊙ Student transcript
⊙ High school profile
⊙ Teacher recommendation letter(s)
  • In some schools teachers upload or submit their own letters
⊙ Mid-year transcripts of first semester grades, in January of senior year
⊙ Final transcripts, after graduation

| APPLICATION TERMINOLOGY | |
|---|---|
| CEEB code | College Entrance Examination Board code is an identification number assigned to differentiate schools. These codes link your high school and college in order to process your application materials and test scores. |
| Early Decision | An application plan in which a student applies to a college early, generally November 1st, and receives a response, generally in December. Check deadlines, however, as the dates vary among colleges. Early Decision is a binding agreement: if a student receives an offer of admission, the student is obliged to accept the offer and to withdraw applications sent to other colleges. |
| Early Action | The same process as early decision, except that a student is not bound to attend and can wait until May 1st to accept the offer of admission. Some colleges allow a student to apply early, but do not allow an applicant to apply to additional schools under an early plan. This plan can be called restrictive early action or early action single choice school. |
| Regular Admission | A plan in which institutions review most of their applications before notifying candidates of their admission. In this process, colleges set a deadline for completing applications and will respond to completed applications by a specified date. |
| Rolling Admission | A process in which applications are evaluated upon receipt and applicants are notified immediately (usually 3-4 weeks) of the decision. |
| Yield | The percentage of students who accept the offer of admission to a college. |

Have a trusted person proofread your application before you submit.

After you submit, colleges will email you a username and password. These will enable you to sign into your individual account, which is your portal for that college. Keep checking each of your college portals to confirm receipt of all documents. Be prepared to receive additional requests from some colleges after submitting.

## START EARLY!
## SUBMIT EARLY!
## DEADLINES MATTER!

# ESSAYS

## Purpose

The other parts of your application show what you've accomplished and experienced and how other people see you. The essay is the only place where you can convey how you see yourself and how you've made meaning of your own experiences.

## Preparing to Write

Collect materials that will help you write about yourself: a list of your extracurricular activities and summer experiences, a list of other experiences that have shaped you as well as notes about why they were influential, a list of people who have influenced you and the impact each made, advice you value, quotes you love, and other words that have deep meaning to you.

## Choosing a Topic

Find essay prompts on the applications and supplements of colleges you are considering, or on the common application. Most prompts address similar themes: an experience that shaped you, a struggle you've overcome, a challenge you've faced, or a person who has influenced you. Pick one. Even if you don't end up applying to that school, the meat of the essay will be transferable to most prompts.

## Pre-writing

Start small. Write down single words or ideas, and then work up to sentences, strings of sentences, and paragraphs. You don't have to start at the beginning. Jump right into the middle, if that is where your ideas are ripest. Take breaks from writing. Returning to the essay with a fresh perspective may help jump-start the writing process after a stall. Repeat until a rough draft is completed.

## Revising

Expect to revise. Once you have a rough draft, you are ready for a second opinion. Ask readers you respect to critique the draft. Readers can be trusted teachers, relatives, coaches, or instructors. Listen to their responses and consider their suggestions, but remember that this essay is yours and should reflect your voice and your thinking.

| TIPS ON CONTENT | TIPS ON STYLE |
|---|---|
| Start with an opening paragraph that captures the reader's interest. | Vary sentence beginnings, lengths, and types. |
| Use a style that feels comfortable and sounds like you. | Use a rich vocabulary but not an unnatural one. Thesaurus-driven essays are easy to spot. |
| Keep your focus narrow. Use a small moment to convey a big idea. | Use action verbs. |
| Show—don't tell—your story. Use detail and imagery to help the reader feel what you felt. Be specific. | The point of view is first person. Use only "I" or "me," not "you" or "one." |
| Write about something you know well. | Read out loud to help with clarity. |
| Avoid clichés and generalizations. | Proofread! |
| Be honest. Reveal yourself. | Proofread! |
| Make sure you have answered the question! | Proofread! |

Mistakes to avoid in the essay include rehashing what is already stated on your application, writing something you think the admissions committee wants to hear, being general—describing the "what" but not explaining the "how" or "why"—and including hyperbole, fiction, distortion, or dishonesty.

As you read your final edition, test it by asking yourself if anybody else's name could go on your essay. It needs to be so specific to you that it could not be anyone else's story.

College officers get pummeled with adjectives, which get lost when they are not embedded in a story. Pull out the vignettes from your experiences that help a reader get to know you. College officers have thousands of applications to review and limited time to accomplish this task—often, they are only able to give each application less than half an hour, and at some schools a mere fifteen minutes. They open the file and see the markings of a final-canoe-race-at-camp essay or my-summer-trip-to-Paris essay, and they nod their heads and say to themselves they have read this essay before. Being generic means you risk losing the opportunity to get the attention of the reader who is trying to get a sense of who you are.

> After reading your essay, admission officers should be able to close their eyes and envision who you are and how you think.

An essay is not a prose version of your resume; your essay is your story, the interpretation of all those past experiences that consolidate and form the person you are becoming. Go beyond merely telling what you did—show how it made you who you are.

## Examples of Essays

Regardless of the prompts, be sure to translate who you have become, how your perspective has changed, or how you have been motivated to take action.

The following excerpts are examples of how you could develop your story in several directions, with different conclusions that are personal to you. Each could be adapted and become an appropriate response to several prompts. Prompts ask for you to write about subjects such as a story central to your identity, a letter to your roommate, websites or books you read, what might influence your major or career path, or an accomplishment.

## Good Opening Sentences

I consider myself a lot of things: [a hacker, an engineer, a math lover, a physics geek;] but above all I have a healthy respect for science of any form.

> **Comment:** Clever opening.

I turned left onto FM 1234 as the sun burnt daylight into the purple haze of dawn. It was 5:15a.m., and I was on my way to a taqueria for my daily dose of breakfast tacos and Dr. Pepper. The thermometer read 80, but I knew by noon it would [sizzle into at least 110.]

> **Comment:** Wonderful description that paints a picture for the reader.

I am curious. Photography has helped me see my world. Photography has helped me communicate what I have seen. Sometimes my camera has been a cushion, insulating me from the pain of human suffering. Sometimes my camera has been a handshake, including me in moments of exultation. But ever since I discovered photography's impact on memory, perception, and communication, my camera has been an extension of my every [experience.]

> **Comment:** How an experience as an artist has adjusted personal perspective.

We live in a world that consists of a series of pictures, all moving at a very rapid pace. I see my job as a photographer to be to capture one of these moments, one of these fleeting seconds in the hustle and bustle of quotidian practices and to hold it up to the world as a statement. [I take seriously] the responsibility that this entails. The way a picture is cropped, the angle of the camera, the way shadows are placed across a scene— each of these techniques evokes a certain effect from an audience. I see my photography as a way to express myself, a way to communicate with the world, a way to sensitize people to issues of [importance.]

> **Comment:** Example of making the art story personal.

> **Comment:** Effective introduction into the detailed content that will follow.

> ## Regardless of content, be sure to answer the question that is asked.

Only one name could go on each of these very personal writing samples. Let these examples help guide your own creative process.

## Highlight A Unique Personality Trait

[I am a news junky.] I listen to NPR every day going to and coming home from school. During school when I have free time in class, I am reading the latest news stories from the Daily Beast or The Huffington Post on my phone. Recently, Newsweek announced it was going digital, and I thought that was a great idea so now I get my subscription of Newsweek on my phone. I have magazine subscriptions to The Economist, Foreign Policy and The New York Times Sunday Edition. I watch Sixty Minutes every Sunday night with my father and Meet the Press if I am up early enough on Sunday. I am half way through a biography on Vladimir Putin that I decided to read because I heard an interview with the author on NPR. I am also listening to and reading the transcripts of secret White House tapes that were recorded during the Kennedy Presidential years that were just released in a book, which I heard about through [Newsweek.]

I bring up current events when talking to friends and family in order to get [their perspective] on the matter. I often quiz my girlfriend and mom on country flags and geography. My friends would tell you I often [spew random facts] of information that I have heard on the news or that is currently being discussed in a conversation. Clearly, my family and friends would describe me as [a news junky.]

**Comment:** Pulling the reader in by suggesting what will come.

**Comment:** This paragraph has excellent examples of using details to support your opening sentence.

**Comment:** Shows open-mindedness and willingness to learn from others without telling us that.

**Comment:** An example of creating a visual image of the writer.

**Comment:** Ties back to original statement.

## THINK DETAILS!

## Showing mastery in your area of study

I want to pursue cyber security for two big reasons. First of all, I simply [enjoy studying the field.] I love tearing any system apart just to see how it works. But secondly, cyber security is really [*really* important]!

**Comment:** Opening identifies preferred area of study.

The biggest problem with cyber security right now is that people tend to blindly put information online and assume it is secure - when that's not always true. For example, do you know what the difference between "HTTP" and "HTTPS" is? Most people don't, but here it is: if you're viewing a website using HTTP, it is easy for some malicious user to see exactly what you do. If you make a purchase using HTTP, your credit card information is transmitted openly. If you're connected to a website using HTTPS though, your connection is secure! Any information sent using HTTPS is between you and the owner of the [website.]

**Comment:** Reasons supporting interest in field of study.

**Comment:** Interesting detail, reader might learn something new, demonstrates awareness of a complicated field.

The solution to this problem seems obvious: use HTTPS. But it's never that easy. In fact, go log on to Facebook right now. Unless you've personally changed your settings to "Browse Facebook on a secure connection (https) when possible" then Facebook will [default to HTTP.]

**Comment:** Translates complex material in an understandable way.

This issue is only one small vulnerability in the wide world of cyber security. As someone who finds studying computers and cyber security very exciting, [I want to pursue a career] in keeping our cyber-interactions safe, preserving the ability for us to share information securely.

**Comment:** Conclusion effective in summarizing topic and making it personally pertinent.

## Supporting a community service outreach with examples specific to the writer

Food is the problem. Information, or the lack of, is an even bigger problem. Obesity is a nationwide [health concern.] My city is listed as one of the fattest cities in America. With fast food growing and American indulgence abounding, food—which keeps a human body alive—can, ironically, lead to many deaths because people simply don't know what food is good for their body or don't have the discipline to make healthy choices. For the past five years, I have been trying to save lives—not in hospitals or in ambulances, but in the streets of [my hometown] and in local high schools.

**Comment:** Catchy opening that defines message to come.

**Comment:** Personal to writer.

I am now president of (put in specific name), an organization dedicated to preventing childhood obesity by teaching children healthy eating habits at a young age. In my freshman year, I led the committee that created a web page where elementary kids could go to learn about basic exercises and healthy eating tips. In my sophomore year, I began speaking at schools and health conventions. My message focused on choosing a healthy lifestyle. My audience expanded from lower school children to teens to teachers to parents. During the summer before my junior year, [I developed a curriculum] for a high school health class, including lesson plans spanning from The Importance of Water to The Implications of Diabetes.

**Comment:** Shows writer's role, and activities personal to writer. Shows quantifiable results from writer's efforts to make a difference.

Through my work, I've learned how lifestyle choices shape health and how health shapes quality of life. My work over the years has inspired me to become a pediatrician; I believe early prevention can offset future health problems such as obesity, which could lead to diabetes or heart disease. From my speaking engagements, I've learned how little people truly know about the implications of their choices—in particular, how little they know about nutrition and the importance of exercise. In the midst of a technological explosion, I find this lack of knowledge upsetting. I realize how much work there is to do informing people on topics from the perils of dehydration to the repercussions of a sedentary lifestyle. [As a pediatrician,] I could do my part to foster better health for future generations.

**Comment:** How the experience has motivated the writer to action. Declaration of a major and a career goal.

## How an activity has changed the way you look at life

As a certified Advanced Open Water scuba diver and avid free diver, I have learned to track and identify fish in their natural habitats and how to explore sunken DC-3 planes from the drug wars and a landing craft from World War II. My expeditions have been self-directed. For example, I have had to teach myself how to identify a fish when the distinguishers like color and anatomy are not obvious because the lack of light in deeper water or places like caves hide them. I have to be able to decide how to react, should I stay or swim away. Sometimes I look at people like this, sometimes who they really are is not so obvious. Free diving has taught me to pay attention to the subtle details that may reveal [the true story.]

**Comment:** Insightful observation about what an activity can teach.

## How an athletic experience adjusted your perspective

In the beginning it was a game, something I started as a freshman and finished four years later. It is amazing how something that was once a simple hobby could become something that touched every aspect of my life. I do not know what I would be like had I—for some reason—been unable to play football. However, of one point I am now certain: I do not follow the crowd—in a sport where guts and skill win the game, you cannot. The ability to lead was not preached any one day, but simply understood and expected of me every day. The whole philosophy was not one I left on the field after practice; it was in the back of my throat when I ate, on the tip of my tongue when I spoke and in my vision when I dreamed. I now realize the toughest challenge was not the 250 pound linebacker I had to block, but rather the attitude with which I faced an approaching obstacle. The field was a testing ground where I left my sweat on the line that prepared me to tackle future adversity. In the end the strength you find along the way to fight your way through defines who you become. What had started as merely a game had, ultimately, [become a way of life.]

> **Comment:** Shows personal growth with descriptive details.

## How an expedition abroad became a point of self-discovery

Boarding the flight to Sao Paulo this past July, I had no idea what to expect from my weeks in Brazil. My mind was brimming with the combination of "Save-the-Rainforest" dogma and ["What-if-I-End-Up-Lost-In-Rio-With-No-Identification"] panic.

**Comment:** Clever.

The team consisted of two school teachers, both young and bilingual, two field researches with a bouncy teething son, and me. Late at night after dinner of stewed beans, white rice, and [guava fruit Tang,] we would link arms and troop down the jeep trail under Southern Hemisphere stars. Looking up through the black Brazilian night, we swapped stories of men and beliefs, [ideals and ideas.]

**Comment:** Attention to detail to engage the reader.

**Comment:** Demonstrates intellectual thought.

During the work day our assignment was to collect data to catalogue the effects of deforestation on the rainforest wildlife. We spent much of our time knee-deep in ferny streams, clutching pencils and listening for blips on the radio tracking devices strapped to our necks. At night we weighed fruit samples, read science journals for information on black fly larvae, and tensely chewed popcorn while watching World Cup soccer, erupting in [hollers of "GOOOOAL!!!" when Brazil scored.]

**Comment:** Paints a picture.

**Comment:** Excellent details.

I returned from Brazil with a passionate enthusiasm for soccer, a taste for exotic Tang, remarkable skills in the [wielding of machetes,] numerous tick welts, and a glimpse of the future. In Brazil I grew up. I met the adult me and we got along like we'd known each other all our lives. I can't tell you that in Brazil I discovered some hidden tap of intellectual bravado, because I didn't. I still long to be intellectually ignited, I still seek for phrases or ideas that twist my perspective into new and interesting shapes, I still thirst to read and write and think about and understand and none of that has anything to do specifically with [Brazil.] But the fact remains that Brazil had a profound effect on my life, I think more in personal growth than in some scholarly epiphany. Show me ideas and I will devour them. Hand me an argument and I will probe it for credibility. Toss me a book and I will bury myself in it. Fly me to a foreign nation and I will immerse myself in it. Point me at a peccary and I will radio track it with no mind of rain or mud or blistered heels. When my mind is ignited, there isn't enough information to feed my senses and thoughts. So in Brazil I ignited myself, and now here I am at home, [burning.]

**Comment:** Example of personal growth.

**Comment:** Strong conclusion that shows how the experience brings clarity to the writer's life.

# RESUMES

Your college resume should enrich and quantify, not merely repeat, what is already on your application. It provides an opportunity to define who you are, to add depth and significant detail to your story, and to be a conversation starter for an interview.

## Purpose

A resume records accomplishments, past responsibilities, special abilities, and specific skills. While the form may vary, the purpose of every resume is ultimately the same: to persuade a college officer or potential employer that you are worthy of his attention. An effective resume should contain descriptive, but succinct, information to tell someone who you are and what you can offer. If your resume is unfocused or poorly organized, people may assume you are too.

## Activity List

Create, build, and save a list of activities as you move through high school. Selective amnesia sets in when you open the application and see all those white spaces! Family and friends can often help fill in the gaps. Look for categories and patterns as you reflect on your life and organize your activities, experiences, and training—your past interests provide clues to potential college majors and future career paths. These moments of self-reflection provide the foundation for self-discovery that will lead you to the best college fit. For those who approach this task thoughtfully, with joyful anticipation about what they might learn about themselves, the rewards are infinite. While you are looking for the right college, you just might find yourself along the way. Life is full of fragmentation and distraction, making it all too easy to forget to pause along our journey and reflect on where we have been and where we are heading. Here is a moment to regroup, redirect, refocus—or focus for the first time—on your life goals, what you stand for, what you really care about. Seize this moment. Grow from it. Tell your story. See the possibilities that await you.

## Describe, Not Disguise

Your resume should describe who you are, not disguise who you are; many applicants confuse these concepts. One word we would like to erase from the college lexicon is "brag sheet"—what a misnomer, laced with arrogance, rather than radiating discovery! Pulling all your past experiences out from memory helps you see the patterns emerging in your life: your interests, your talents, and your exposure to places and ideas. Students mistakenly think that if they have not started an orphanage in Africa, sent Sox-in-a-Box to homeless children in Costa Rica, or worked with a big-name firm on Wall Street they will not get into a selective college. Applicants think readers are calculating how abundant or spectacular the items on their resume might be. Most students list their activities, but neglect to explain who they have become through these experiences.

A savvy applicant will be thoughtful about creating a guided reading experience for the over-worked reader by using descriptive headings and quantifying depth of commitment in short clips. Help your reader get to know who you are quickly. Describe, don't disguise—no puffing, no padding. College application readers can see through paid-for, passive activities. While expensive, glamorous summer experiences can be genuine catalysts for personal growth, many students go into them thinking having them appear on their resume will assure their admission. Your story should go beyond merely relating what you have done. Be sure you feature how you immersed yourself and how you developed from the experience. Tell the story of your genuine growth.

| THE BASICS | |
| --- | --- |
| **Paper** (for when you need a hard copy beyond an electronic submission): | White or off-white, heavyweight, 100% rag content bond is always safe. Avoid abnormal colors or design-laden paper. |
| **Font** | Make sure your font is readable—usually Times New Roman works well. |
| **Heading** | Always include your name and email address. A job or internship resume should also carry your home address and phone number; a college resume only needs your email address. |
| **Format** | This area gets tricky. A format that looks great for one student might look terrible for another. The format depends on what you have done. If you have particular depth in one area—academics, athletics, arts, or clubs—your resume should reflect the strength in those areas by creating descriptive category headings for those sections. Graphically, as in any effective advertisement, the important part of what you wish to sell should be up front—at the top of your resume. The rest of what occurs should be designed to make what is written as impressive and attractive as possible. |

| | |
|---|---|
| Activity Description | Within the format you have selected, how you say what you have done is as important as where you place it. You should attempt to tell not only what you did, but also how well you did it and perhaps even what you became as a result of it. Use a staccato style of writing, with a generous use of action verbs as statement lead-ins. Use numbers, adverbs, and anecdotes to illustrate your competence. Make statements positive, result-oriented, and aggressive. Mention time saved, dollars earned, items produced, people served, and pages written. The people making the ultimate decisions about you respond to quantified details. Remember each verb you use represents a skill. |
| Special Skills and Interests | After a while, resumes start to look the same to a recruiter or a college officer. You can often personalize your resume through this section. It is more interesting to say you ran the New York Marathon in 3:55 than to say your interests include jogging. Unique hobbies or unique accomplishments go here, again with succinct details and action verbs. |
| Length | Business resumes should be one page only. College resumes can go to two pages if absolutely necessary. Keep in mind that a resume is neither an autobiographical essay nor a detailed list of everything you have ever done. Rank-order items you will include. Be truthful and accurate, remembering that you can emphasize certain points that you feel will distinguish you. |

> This process rewards those who enter it with conviction and take the time to think deeply.

## Sample Resumes

The following entries provide examples of how to quantify the extent of time you committed to a program, project, or training, the number of people served, the depth of commitment, or the level of mastery.

**What not to do:**

EXTRACURRICULAR ACTIVITIES
⊙ Community service—grades 9, 10, 11, 12

This heading and line item are too general and miss the opportunity to guide your reader to an immediate impression of who you are and what you have accomplished.

> Think details and
> be specific.

**COMMUNITY SERVICE OUTREACH: SERVICE TO CHILDREN**

Crusaders against Cancer – grades 11, 12

*Founder of club that raised $100,000 for lymphoma research*

Buddy Ball – grades 10, 11, 12

*Coached team with fifteen players in a basketball league for physically and mentally challenged kids weekly October – February*

**JOURNALISM TRAINING AND EXPERIENCES**

School Magazine – grades 10, 11, Editor-in-Chief 12

*School news magazine: staff writer—world news columnist; responsibilities as editor-in-chief include writing and editing copy, designing layout*

**INTERNATIONAL EXPERIENCES**

Hamburg, Germany: summer following grade 9

Rotary Club Youth Exchange

*Homestay with German family and hosted German student, one month each; participated in daily classes for language immersion, explored cultural and historical landmarks, interacted with families through excursions*

**FINE ARTS: PHOTOGRAPHY**

Art Institute State Competition – 1st place

*Statewide juried exhibit with 350 applicants*

City Newspaper – published photographs

*Monthly contributor to real-estate department*

Photographic Business

*Established my own photographic business: custom invitations, holiday portraits, website pictures, photography of ranch properties for marketing*

**ATHLETICS: SPECIALTY TRAINING**

Tae Kwon Do – age 6 to present

*Earned a second degree black belt*

*Qualified to try out for the Olympic team*

*Learned self-discipline and integrity through all my years of training*

# LETTERS OF RECOMMENDATION

Letters of recommendation are a strong factor in the overall decision to admit a student. Admission officers seek to synthesize academic and personal qualities through comments from people who know a student best. These observations can reveal what cannot be captured in grades and scores.

## College Counselor Recommendations

The college counselor's role is to provide supplementary documents:
- Secondary School Report form
- Transcript
- High school profile to give context for the transcript
- Letter of recommendation

The counselor's letter helps to bring the student to life as the thinking, feeling person behind the numbers. Take time to know your counselor and provide the details needed to support your application. Share your story.

## Teacher Recommendations

Teacher letters provide useful information about you that will provide admission offices with an accurate interpretation of your academic record and potential. Colleges generally request recommendations from teachers who taught you during your junior or senior year. Colleges are looking for evidence of intellectual curiosity, a mind at work, initiative, and leadership. Teachers' recommendations will address your performance, demeanor, and character in the classroom.

Performance: How do you…
- Learn best
- Keep pace with the workload of the course
- Compare with other students in the class
- Measure up to personal potential

Demeanor: How do you…
⊙ Interact with peers
⊙ Participate in class discussion
⊙ Interact with teachers or other adults
⊙ Respond to setbacks or challenges
⊙ Handle stress
⊙ Feel about learning

Character: What are your…
⊙ Passions
⊙ Distinguishers
⊙ Salient characteristics (e.g. humor, fairness, honesty, creativity, competitiveness)
⊙ Most valuable contributions to the learning environment

## Supplemental Recommendations

If you have an area of particular accomplishment or talent, it can be appropriate to have an additional letter from the person who knows you in that context and can quantify your level of expertise or contribution. These recommenders can provide further insight into your performance, character, and demeanor in an area that may be more comfortable and is more distinct than the classroom setting. These letters are generally sent directly to the colleges.

## Alumni Recommendations

These letters can be appropriate and effective if the person knows you or your family well and can express why you would be a particularly good fit for the college. Because alumni know both the college and the applicant, their perspective can be helpful and can validate a potential fit.

> Any recommendation is only as good as how well a person knows you. Colleges want good people, not just good grades!

## Sample Letters of Recommendation

Colleges are looking to your teachers and those who know you best to learn about whether you will be a good fit for their programs. Colleges are looking for intellectual curiosity and how you tackle academic material. You need to get to know your recommenders and help them get to know you in order to help them write the letter that will help the college admission readers decide if you are the applicant they are looking for to enrich their community. The following comments suggest ways that recommenders can share how they know you best—how they can provide insight on how you think, describe your work ethic, validate your talents, and attest to your resilience—and move you toward landing the seat at the college that fits you.

Here are some examples of letters of recommendation. Look at the ways these teachers describe their students, and think about the teachers who would have the best ability to describe you in this depth.

*Kathy is a creative force in my English class. She always finds ways to improve every paragraph, every story, every play she creates or encounters. She has a problem with mediocrity. Her critiques of her peers' work are insightful and kind, yet she remains ever vigilant about preserving the feelings of less gifted writers. Kathy is a brilliant writer herself who demonstrates moments of true genius. She is a lively conversationalist, as well, frequently sharing her responses to recent literary readings she has attended and new novels she has just finished...*

*Behind Paul's rough and tumble exterior as a seasoned athlete, there sits a remarkably sensitive and articulate young man, indeed a poet. An avid reader and conscientious student, Paul sits each year on the esteemed committee that determines the summer reading lists for the school. His suggestions are taken seriously. He shared with me that in his personal reading, Paul gravitates most frequently to biographies of warriors...*

*Peter works with diligence in my math class, readily solving some of the most complex problem sets. When he is pushed with particularly challenging or new material, he keeps at it until he reaches a reasonable answer—and then seeks counsel to confirm his answer or look for more resources to master the concept. I know Peter primarily as his math teacher, but in a recent conversation with him I discovered what many in our school do not know: Peter has a voluminous repertoire of musical knowledge. He plays the clarinet, the piano by ear, and composes prodigiously. He shared with me that he has composed a piano concerto, a minuet and an overture...*

*An example of the behind-the-scenes support Steve brings to our school is seen in the athletic department where he works as a trainer with the varsity football team...*

*Computer and guru and problem solver, Josh is the one the teachers and staff seek out when they encounter a technical glitch with their computers...*

> **Write a thank-you note to anyone who writes a recommendation for you.**

# COLLEGE INTERVIEWS

Many colleges make an interview an official part of the application process. Some colleges will not grant personal interviews because they do not have enough staffers to handle the volume of candidates and they are reluctant to give an unfair advantage to those who are positioned near their campus. Most colleges will offer an online video interview option. Colleges also provide an opportunity for applicants to meet with representatives of the school, generally current students or local alumni, for an information exchange. In any case, these interactions provide a forum for a student to clarify procedures and expectations, as well as for a college to promote its programs.

Under whatever circumstances an interview may occur, certain protocol is always appropriate.

⊙ Arrive on time.
⊙ Wear appropriate clothing. You can only make a first impression once.
⊙ Research and prepare questions in advance that cannot be readily answered by perusing the college website.
⊙ Introduce your parents and then go into the interview alone.
⊙ Be ready to discuss your accomplishments, your interests, and your goals with appropriate humility and expressive detail.
⊙ Include somewhere in the conversation why you think you would be a good fit for the college. Pull on your research and be specific.
⊙ Remember to be a good listener. Maintain eye contact and a positive demeanor.
⊙ Thank-you notes will always be appreciated and remembered.

Use the interview as an opportunity to learn about the college and express your interest in it. This is your chance to personalize your application.

## Questions an Interviewer Might Ask

Reflect on the following questions in preparation for your interview, remembering that your interviewer is trying to get to know you better to see if you are the right fit for their school.

- ⊙ What interests you about our college?
- ⊙ What would you like to study in college?
- ⊙ What would you bring to a college community?
- ⊙ What recent book have you read and how did it change the way you think?
- ⊙ What is your favorite activity?
- ⊙ How have you spent your summers?
- ⊙ What is the most significant contribution you have made to your school?
- ⊙ What would you say is one your greatest strengths and weaknesses as a student? As a person?
- ⊙ What are your long-term career goals?
- ⊙ What event in the world has you thinking right now about it?
- ⊙ What would you like to share with me so that I can present your strongest case to our admission committee?

# DEMONSTRATED INTEREST

Colleges monitor the level of an applicant's interest in order to determine the probability that you will actually enroll if accepted. Since many students who apply to highly competitive institutions have top academic achievement and exemplary personal accomplishment, a college dean can look to demonstrated interest as a potential tiebreaker. Colleges may or may not disclose that they use demonstrated interest as a factor.

### How do colleges track demonstrated interest?

- College Fair visits
- Campus visits
- Requests for information directly from college
  - Are you on the mailing list?
- Contact with your admission representative
- Response to communications from the college (opening your email indicates interest)
- Sending a thank-you note—paper or email
- Applying early
- Completion of supplemental essays (optional is never optional)
- Attending sessions at your high school when college representative visits
- Interview
- Calls to the admissions office asking to speak to a professor
- Checking portals

### How can you further demonstrate your interest?

In the college essay that asks why you're interested in this school, clearly articulate why the school is a good match, even if you fit the profile exactly. The admissions reader needs to see the details of why you are a good fit and understand the care you have taken to determine what a good match you are for that particular school. Think of your essay as an interview, and use it wisely to define how well you would fit.

- Read journal articles from professors and school newspapers and quote the stories.

⊙ Inform a college if you have been on the campus—for example:
  • Go to a football game
  • Attend a summer program
  • Visit current students who are friends

Also remember:

⊙ Make sure emails and phone calls to the school or representative are from you, not your parent.

⊙ Use appropriate aggression—do not become a stalker!

⊙ Know your audience and communicate appropriately.

In all your communications with the school, avoid being inappropriate. Use conventional grammar and spelling, not what is used in texts and social media. Double-check grammar, punctuation, and spelling. Make sure your email address is appropriate. It may feel like a casual email, but it will become a permanent part of your file.

> **DO YOUR RESEARCH.**
> Be prepared with appropriate details
> in your correspondence and essays.

# SPECIAL INTERESTS
## Fine Arts and Theater

If you want to be an artist, a filmmaker, a photographer, a dancer, a theater star, or a musician or if you want to major or minor in any kind of arts department, there will be a few more steps to your application.

Look closely at the requirements for each school. Some will have unique deadlines and often an additional essay.

Each school can differ in
- How they want you to submit a portfolio
- What they are looking for in a portfolio
- When they want you to do an audition
- What they want you to sing or perform

> **Assume you will need to provide a portfolio or give an audition.**

## National Portfolio Days: www.portfolioday.net

National Portfolio Days offer an opportunity for visual artists and designers to meet with representatives from colleges accredited by the National Association of Schools of Art and Design who will review your artwork, discuss their programs, and answer questions about professional careers in art. High school students, parents, teachers, guidance counselors, and college transfer students may attend.

National Portfolio Days are also about the exchange of information about your work, yourself, your college plans, and your concerns. It is not an examination or a competition. Your portfolio should include your best and most recent work, but it can also include works in progress, sketchbooks, and tear sheets.

Some colleges represented may accept your portfolio as the visual portion of your application. Other colleges have restrictions that prohibit them from making a definite portfolio decision at the time of your review. Discuss your work with as many representatives as possible, and expect different responses to your work.

Make sure you keep a copy of everything you submit!

Majors and Concentrations for National Portfolio Day:

| | |
|---|---|
| Accessories Design | Combined Degree |
| Advertising | Comic Illustration/Cartooning |
| Advertising Design | Communication/Communication Design |
| Animation | Community Arts |
| Applied Theatre Arts | Computer Graphics/Arts |
| Architecture | Crafts (Ceramics, Fibers, Jewelry & Metalsmithing) |
| Art Education | Creative Writing |
| Art History | Critical Theory |
| Art Therapy | Culture and Politics |
| Arts Administration | Curatorial Practices |
| Bachelor of Science (BSc): Entrepreneurial Studies | Design and Technology |
| Book Arts | Design Criticism |
| Broadcasting | Digital Film |
| Business/Business of Art & Design | Digital Photography |
| Ceramics | Digital/Electronics Media |
| Clay | Display and Exhibit Design |

| | |
|---|---|
| Drawing | Jewelry |
| Electronic Arts | Landscape Architecture |
| Enameling | Liberal Arts & Sciences |
| Entertainment Design | Literary Studies |
| Environmental Design | Medical Illustration |
| Environmental Public Art | Menswear |
| Exhibition and Museum Studies | Metals |
| Fashion Design | Multimedia |
| Fibers/Textiles | Neon |
| Film | Painting |
| Fine Arts | Papermaking |
| Furniture Design | Performance Production |
| Game Design | Performance/New Genres |
| Gender Studies | Performing Arts (Music, Dance, Theater) |
| Glass | Photo Design |
| Graphic Design | Photo Journalism |
| Historical Preservation | Photography |
| History of Decorative Arts | Post Baccalaureate Program |
| Illustration | Printing/Publishing |
| Industrial Design | Printmaking |
| Installation Art | Product Design |
| Interdisciplinary Arts | Public Art |
| Interior Design/Interior Architecture | Scientific Illustration |
| Intermedia/Interactive Media | Screenprinting |

| Sculpture | Transportation Design |
|---|---|
| Self-Designed Major | Urban Studies |
| Sonic/Sound Art | Video |
| Studio Art | Visual Communications/Studies/Design |
| Surface Pattern Design | Web Design |
| Theater Design | Wood/Wood Design/Woodworking/Furniture |
| Time-Based Media | Writing |
| Toy Design | |

## Sports in College

If athletics have been important in your high school experience, you may want to continue your participation. There are several ways to play sports in college.

**Intramurals:** These are recreational sports teams organized within the college. You sign up for these once you are attending the college.

**Club:** Club sports compete competitively with other colleges, but they are not regulated by the NCAA or a similar intercollegiate athletic association. If you are interested in continuing your sport at the club level, reach out to current players and coaches before you apply to a school to learn more about the team. They may be able to put in a good word for you in admissions—at some schools your sport may only exist at the club level—but they will still not recruit with scholarships for the team.

### NCAA: National Collegiate Athletic Association

**Division I** – Schools ranked as D1 by the NCAA generally have large student bodies, have significant athletic budgets, and provide the most scholarships.

To play DI, you must be eligible through the NCAA Clearinghouse and follow specific rules for recruitment. If you are a DI athletic recruit, you will probably know where you are going to college earlier than your senior year.

**Division II** – DII is a collection of 300 NCAA colleges that provide student-athletes the opportunity to compete at a high level of scholarship athletics while excelling in the classroom and fully engaging in the broader campus experience. It offers an alternative to both the highly competitive level of intercollegiate sports offered in NCAA Division I and to the no athletic scholarship option offered in Division III.

To play for a DII school, you must be eligible through the NCAA Clearinghouse and follow specific rules for recruitment.

**Division III** – DIII is the largest NCAA division, by both number of students and schools. The primary focus for DIII student-athletes is academics. DIII schools have shorter practice and playing seasons and regional competition that reduces time away from academic studies. Student-athletes take part in the experiences of the regular student body. DIII schools do not offer specific athletic scholarships to their student-athletes. You do not have to be eligible through the NCAA Clearinghouse, but you can be recruited. Although these colleges cannot give scholarship money for playing on a team, you can get financial aid or another academic scholarship.

To play DIII sports, you do not need to register with the NCAA.

**Recruitment**
The best source for helping athletes through the recruitment process is the NCAA Eligibility Center website. Under their resource tab, you can find the GPA/Test Score Scale, the recruiting rules by sport, and just about anything else you need to know about what NCAA is and what you need to be eligible to play in college. They are very willing to talk if you call with questions.

The next best source for learning about the recruitment process is your high school coach. Your school may put on recruitment information evenings to provide you with information. You can try to talk with a college coach, but he or she will be less transparent than the high school coach.

The first step in being recruited is to put together a sports resume and video clip. You can provide a link to a website you create or to a YouTube video. Your video has to be only a click away or college coaches may not take the time to look.

Once you have put together a sports resume and video clip to share, you need to start visiting schools and contacting coaches. It is best if one of your high school or club coaches contacts college coaches—either at schools you have targeted or ones where they have contacts. If your coaches don't have time or don't seem interested in helping, you will need to reach out yourself.

You should also attend athletic weekends and organized recruitment events where groups of coaches go in order to watch players.

There are specific recruiting/contacting dates, so each student needs to look up when and where they can meet with coaches. A general rule is that students can reach out to coaches anytime, but coaches have to reach out to students within specific dates. Coaches also have limitations as to how many phone calls, texts, and personal contacts they can make with a player. You must follow these protocols.

## The College Search

The biggest decision when it comes to playing NCAA sports will be

⊙ Do you want to choose a college and then go after the coaches?

or

⊙ Do you want to see who recruits you and go where they want you to play?

The best strategy is to do both. Even if you choose the second option, you need to visit schools in your area to see the differences in the big ones and the small ones and get to know the unique aspects of each school. If you pick a college based on a coach, you will still be attending the school for four years! So, you want to be able to choose the school that fits you best.

Sometimes coaches will ask athletes to apply early decision or early action. If you are asked to submit your application this way, make sure to follow those guidelines and deadlines accurately.

When a DI school is interested in you, you may receive:

⊙ **A letter of intent** – an agreement between the college and the student athlete saying you will play for that college and that they will grant you an athletic scholarship, or
⊙ **A likely letter** – a letter from the college demonstrating their interest in you, generally offering an "early read" by the admission committee and, hopefully, offering an early acceptance to the school and designated athletic program.

Always confirm whether or not any scholarship you are offered would remain valid if you sustain an injury.

### What is the NCAA Eligibility Center? Why is it Important?

The National Collegiate Athletic Association Eligibility Center took over operations for the NCAA Initial-Eligibility Clearinghouse in November 2007. The Eligibility Center certifies the academic and amateur credentials of all students who want to play sports at an NCAA Division I or II institution as freshmen. In order to practice, play, and receive an athletic scholarship, students need to meet certain academic benchmarks. An additional certification process exists to make sure the student is still an amateur, which is necessary in order for the student to compete.

*Academic Credentials + Amateurism Status = College Eligible*

If you are pursuing Division I or II schools, you need to register with the NCAA Eligibility Center, preferably by your sophomore year in high school. The Eligibility Center is where coaches can find you. You will need to have your high school send in official transcripts, and you will need to send in your SAT/ACT test scores by using the testing center code of 9999. For some sports, like football and basketball, coaches cannot make a high school visit to the student unless that student has submitted test scores.

The Eligibility Center goes through your high school courses and confirms you have the core courses you need. A core GPA combines with SAT/ACT test scores to meet the academic eligibility requirement, with a sliding scale. If you have a higher GPA, you can have a lower test score, or vice versa.

**What are the Academic Initial-Eligibility Requirements?**
The following requirements must be met in order for you to be able to practice, play, and receive a scholarship at an NCAA Division I or II college or university.

**Division I:**
- ⊙ Graduate from high school
- ⊙ Complete the minimum number of core courses
- ⊙ Present the required grade-point average (GPA) (see the sliding scale in the Guide for the College-Bound Student-Athlete for Division I on the website)
- ⊙ Present a qualifying test score on either the ACT or SAT (see the sliding scale in the Guide for the College-Bound Student-Athlete)
- ⊙ Complete the amateurism questionnaire and request final amateurism certification.

**Division I Core-Course Breakdown:** Courses must appear on your list of approved core courses.
- 4 years of English
- 3 years of math (Algebra 1 or higher)
- 2 years of natural or physical science (including one year of lab science if offered by your high school)
- 1 extra year of English, math, or natural or physical science
- 2 years of social science
- 4 years of extra core courses from any category above, foreign language, or nondoctrinal/comparative religion/philosophy

**Division II:**
- ⊙ Graduate from high school
- ⊙ Complete a minimum of core courses
- ⊙ Present the required grade-point average (GPA) (see the sliding scale in the Guide for the College-Bound Student-Athlete for Division II)
- ⊙ Present a qualifying test score on either the ACT or SAT (see the sliding scale in the Guide for the College-Bound Student-Athlete)
- ⊙ Complete the amateurism questionnaire and request final amateurism certification.

**Division II Core-Course Breakdown:** Courses must appear on your list of approved core courses.
- 3 years of English
- 2 years of math (Algebra 1 or higher)
- 2 years of natural or physical science (including one year of lab science if offered by your high school)
- 2 additional years of English, math, or natural or physical science (3 years required in 2013 and beyond)
- 2 years of social science
- 3 years of extra core courses from any category above, or foreign language, nondoctrinal/comparative religion/philosophy (4 years required in 2013 and beyond)

### Important Things to Remember

⊙ The NCAA will NOT count a fifth year of high school; the clock stops after four years of high school.

⊙ You must complete a specific number of core courses prior to beginning senior year or they will not be counted as eligible.

⊙ Only core courses like English, Math, and Science will count towards your GPA.

The NCAA will review your final transcript following high school graduation and grant eligibility if all requirements are met. Any questions will result in an audit. Be prepared to produce handwritten notes, papers you wrote, and completed assignments throughout high school.

### Online Schools

Some athletes chose to attend virtual, online high schools. If this is your situation, make sure your institution is NCAA approved before you start classes. And, as with any type of high school, it is essential for you to keep good records of your education to accommodate a potential future audit.

### Navigating the NCAA Eligibility Center Website

www.eligibilitycenter.org

⊙ Go to the high school administration section.

⊙ Go to the Resources Tab where you will find all the information broken into sections.

Start at the website and click on the cell phone to start your registration. Register and pay with a credit card, then you can go back and continue to login and check who has been looking at you and how your file is doing in the review process.

**Remember:** Never accept gifts from coaches.

# PAYING
## FOR
# COLLEGE

C olleges try to meet your demonstrated financial need. Colleges expect you and your family to contribute as much as you can to the cost of your education. However, they will do their best to bridge the gap between what you can afford and what the college costs. Therefore, consider colleges regardless of the cost of attendance (COA), as aid may be available that could make enrolling at a more expensive school affordable. Financial aid packages can vary from school to school.

You can negotiate final financial terms with each college to which you have been accepted by communicating directly with the financial aid officers.

| FINANCIAL TERMINOLOGY | |
|---|---|
| Cost of attendance (COA) | Tuition costs as well as costs for housing, food, books, transportation, and other daily living expenses. Try to estimate your COA to prepare for determining your financial needs. |
| Expected Family Contribution (EFC) | The amount your family is officially expected to contribute to the cost of your education, as generated from the information you provide on the FAFSA, or Free Application for Federal Student Aid. Many variables that affect a family's financial situation are considered in determining the EFC, including annual income, number of children in college, number of people living in the house, state of residence, age of parents, and types of assets and savings. |
| Forms: FAFSA, PROFILE, Institution Specific Applications | Many colleges require the FAFSA. It should be filed January 1st of the senior year or as close thereafter as possible. The customized institutional PROFILE is required by many colleges, and can be filed after September 15th of the senior year. The PROFILE uses additional information including home equity, regional differences in cost of living, private school tuition, and extraordinary medical expenses so they can be more responsive to family needs. FAFSA and PROFILE forms are available online. Pay close attention to deadlines. |
| Financial Need | A student's financial need is the difference between the EFC and the COA at a college or university. Need-based financial awards are based on this amount. Net Price Calculators are available on individual college websites to help you estimate cost of attendance. |
| Merit-based aid | Financial aid awarded on the basis of factors other than financial need, such as academic performance or special artistic or athletic talents. |

| Need-blind admissions | Policy of reviewing applications for admissions without regard to applicants' financial needs. This policy protects students who have financial need from discrimination in the admissions process. After an admission decision has been made, the college's financial aid staff reviews the student's application for financial aid and creates its aid package. |
|---|---|
| Need-based aid | Financial aid awarded on the basis of the financial need shown by a family, determined by the FAFSA and the PROFILE for the colleges that require it. |

## Track deadlines closely.

# PROCESS
### Applying for Financial Assistance

1. Apply for admission to the college before the admission application deadline.
2. Apply for financial aid in accordance with deadlines. File the FAFSA as soon as possible after January 1st and any other required forms; some colleges may require the institutional PROFILE, as well—the PROFILE can often be filed earlier in the semester. It is to your advantage to apply early, while colleges have available funds. Consider filing both the FAFSA and the PROFILE regardless of financial need, as some colleges may reference these forms for distributing institutional and merit aid. If you *really don't* need financial assistance, you do not need to check the box or fill out the forms.
3. The admission committee meets and grants admission.
4. The college's financial office reviews the application for financial aid.
5. Candidates are notified by the admission office of acceptance. At the same time, or shortly thereafter, the financial aid office notifies candidates of the financial award being offered.

## TYPES OF FINANCIAL ASSISTANCE

| | |
|---|---|
| Scholarships and Grants | Outright gifts most commonly awarded based on need, but sometimes based on academic excellence or special talents. This kind of aid includes institutional scholarships and grants, corporate scholarships, Federal Pell Grants, and the Federal Supplementary Educational Opportunity Grant (SEOG). |
| Loans | A significant part of most aid packages. Typically, they have lower interest rates than other types of loans and don't need to be repaid until after graduation. Types of loans available include institutional loans, student loans (including the Federal Perkins loan and Stafford Subsidized and Unsubsidized Loans), and parent loans (including the federal PLUS loan). |
| Work-Study Programs | Programs that provide funds to students in exchange for working part-time, usually on campus. Federal College Work-Study Employment (CWS) is need-based, but colleges often offer student employment of their own, which is not need-based. |
| 529 Savings Plans | Plans that allow families to pay now for future tuition. Every state has a Section 529 plan. There are two forms: Prepaid Tuition Plans and College Savings Plans. Research carefully the pros and cons to decide what might be appropriate for your family. |
| Community Service | The federal government may cancel all or part of an education loan when the borrower participates in a loan forgiveness program, such as Americorps, Teach for America, or Peace Corps after graduation. |

# WHAT
## INTERNATIONAL
# STUDENTS
## NEED TO KNOW

American schools welcome international students. Colleges recognize the importance of creating a global community. International students will follow the same procedures as American students with additional requirements, which can vary from college to college. Pay attention to details and deadlines.

American higher education uses a "holistic" approach for making decisions to admit students to its colleges. Unlike most other countries, there is no national exam that defines a student's future educational options. While the SAT or ACT play a role, additional items are taken into consideration, such as additional tests, essays, activities, school reports, letters of recommendation, and certificates of finance. Each college may ask for different information, depending on its institutional priorities, so search the website or talk to an admission officer for particular details. International students must follow the steps in previous sections, and have additional information to gather. It can't be emphasized enough: *Start early!*

Another difference that international families face is the difference in focus. American colleges have programs in liberal arts versus the professional programs that most other countries use to educate their undergraduates. While engineering, technology, and business are certainly popular courses of study, American higher education encourages students to explore a variety of disciplines. One discipline will become a concentrated major and some students add a different area for an double major or minor. The goal is to find a program that is a good fit for each student to maximize individual productivity in a future career by learning how to research, analyze, and communicate. Companies are now looking for students who are creative problem solvers. Liberal arts programs can expose students to a wide range of ideas and historical contexts that can enrich their technical training, making them more competitive in the job market or for a graduate school program.

Be aware of your expectations. Many families look at the prestige of a school, rather than at personal fit. There are many college names familiar to the world. Yet there are many options beyond the obvious where students can find success.

### Learning about American Colleges and Universities

Each college designates international admission representatives who spend most of their year traveling abroad to different high schools to meet students interested in attending college in the United States. It is very important to watch for the times when college representatives will be in your area and meet them. After they visit, they will communicate with you primarily through email. Meeting you in person will help them put your face to your file. They want to determine if you speak English well enough to be in a classroom without an interpreter and are able to participate in class discussions. If this describes you, meeting the representative can help you. If you do not have the opportunity to meet anyone, you should reach out to the college admissions officers and try to set up an online interview.

## AMERICAN HIGHER EDUCATION OFFERS MANY OPTIONS

| | |
|---|---|
| Dual Degree | Combining two distinct degree types; two degrees and two diplomas are awarded. An example is combining the degrees of Bachelor of Science in Chemistry and Bachelor of Fine Arts. |
| Double Major | Combining two distinct majors under the same degree; only one degree is awarded. An example is earning a Bachelor of Science in Chemistry and Biology |
| Self-Designed Major | A student designs the major, often across disciplines, to achieve a particular goal: combining business, technology, education, and art may be perfect for a student who might want to create a unique online business. |
| Minor | A minor is a second area of concentration with fewer hours of courses than a designated major that allows a student to add depth to his training and profile. |
| Concentration | Within a major, a student can specify an area of study. For example, a student could major in International Policy with a concentration in the Middle East. |

**Alert:** Avoid using nicknames on documents when filling out forms and applications. Be sure you use the exact same name on all documents to avoid confusion and the potential for misfiled paperwork. Most schools will not combine papers with names that do not match your passport and visa.

**Points to Consider**

You may have culture shock upon arrival at an American school. When you are exploring colleges, ask yourself these questions:

- ⊙ How does the school support international students once they are on campus?
- ⊙ What academic support is available?
- ⊙ What kind of social services will you be able to access?
- ⊙ Will having extended family in the area be important to you?
- ⊙ Do you need a peer group of international students to feel comfortable?

## Submitting the Application

### Transcripts and Academic Records

School records from your past four years need to be officially translated into English and should be submitted directly from the schools in a sealed envelope. You may also send any national testing results. All documents needing to be translated into English should be translated by a certified translator and notarized.

### Testing

Plan to take the **SAT** and/or the **ACT**. In addition, most colleges will require an **English Proficiency Test** such as the **TOEFL** or the **IELTS**. Colleges look for proof of English language proficiency, especially if English is your second language or if your high school education was not in the United States. Some colleges offer conditional admission based on English language proficiency.

**TOEFL – TEST OF ENGLISH AS A FOREIGN LANGUAGE:** The TOEFL measures English language skills in speaking, reading, writing, and listening.

**IELTS – INTERNATIONAL ENGLISH LANGUAGE TESTING SYSTEM:** The IELTS measures English language skills in speaking, reading, writing, and listening; the speaking session is with a live person.

### Letters of Recommendation

In many countries, letters of recommendation are not standard, so you may have to identify your potential writers and help them understand that American schools are looking for your intellectual potential and accomplishments. In the end, it is your responsibility to provide this additional information, which can be pivotal as college officers make decisions to admit. If the people you are asking do not speak English, a certified translation will be required.

### Certification of Finances

This form—available on college websites—standardizes financial information provided by applicants and is a prerequisite in obtaining a **Certificate of Eligibility, Form I-20** (available on college websites), after a student is admitted to a college. Many colleges will not read an application until this form is received. Strict government regulations, rising educational costs, and economic conditions have made verification of financial resources of international applicants essential. Financial aid is limited for international students since they are not eligible for federal funding. Some countries issue a list of schools to which their government will contribute partial or full costs.

### Certificate of Eligibility, Form I-20
The Form I-20 is issued by your hosting school after they grant you admission. You must take your I-20 with you when you apply for your visa.

### Passport
You will need to submit a copy of your passport, including your photo. If you have dual citizenship with the United States, you will be considered an American applicant.

### Visa
If you are already in the United States, you will need to submit your visa information, plus a copy of the photo. If you are applying from another country, you need to obtain a student visa. Know your visa restrictions, specifically for travel and employment. For further information, go to www.unitedstatesvisas.gov to learn more about your visa.

## A Note about Plagiarism:
The deliberate use of someone else's work, words, or ideas without acknowledging the source is an academic offense in American higher education, subject to potential expulsion. Colleges consider plagiarism a serious offense.

# AFTER
## THE
# DECISIONS
## COME IN

**April 1st** – Most college decisions should be out by portals, email, or mail
**May 1st** – the National Candidate Reply Date to accept one college

## PROCEDURES TO FOLLOW

- By May 1st, accept the offer and submit a deposit. You must deposit at *one* American school even if you are still waiting for decisions from other countries.
- If you miss the May 1st deadline, you might forfeit your admission.
- Do not double deposit.
- Notify the colleges whose offers you will not be accepting.
- Send thank-you notes to those who helped support your application, and let them know where you plan to attend.
- Send in housing forms.
- Send in roommate forms.
- Complete any further financial aid documentation by deadline.
- Keep up your grades, and don't get suspended, expelled, or arrested. Colleges can rescind their offer to you.

## NAVIGATING THE WAITLIST

Students who are not initially accepted to a college are sometimes placed on a waiting list. Institutions extend to a student the possibility of admission in the future, after they know how many applicants have accepted their offer. If spaces in the incoming class remain open, the college may then offer admission to students placed on the waiting list, usually between May and July of the senior year. If you land on the waiting list, consider adding one or more of the following to your application file:

⊙ An additional recommendation letter by someone who has not written for you before
⊙ Update of grades – if they indicate a significant upward change
⊙ Update if anything new happened senior year
⊙ Email saying you will come if they find a spot for you! (Only if it is true.)

Some colleges request a response from you to hold a place on their waitlist. Even if you accept a position on a waitlist, you still must make a deposit at another college to have a guaranteed spot in the fall. If you have deposited and then get accepted off a waitlist at a school you prefer to attend, you inform the first college and forfeit that deposit, then make a deposit at the school to which you have been newly accepted.

## GAP YEAR

Once admitted, some students choose to defer starting college for a year in order to pursue a special interest, develop a special talent, or participate in an extended service project. A student must accept the offer of admission, send in a deposit, and then request a deferral. Check individual school policies about specific requirements.

# WHY
## THE ADMISSION
# PROCESS
## IS SO COMPLEX

E scalating numbers of applicants have clogged the college admission pipeline. The electronic application means that more students can apply to more colleges. A commitment to diversity coupled with the redistribution of financial aid has provided access and affordability to many students who formerly did not bother to apply. Recent economic turbulence has sent many people back to college to prepare for career shifts. Because admission officers use a "holistic approach" to review applicants, admission decisions appear to be subjective, often reflecting institutional needs which can vary from institution to institution and from year to year, and are unpredictable.

How do you best approach the process? *Find out exactly who you are and what you want before you apply.* Honest self-assessment takes time. Figuring out your personal goals and individual patterns will help you make the best possible choices. With clarity of purpose, you can avoid making decisions based on stereotypes. College choice is a process that rewards those who pay attention to nuance. *Don't worry if you don't know who you will be when you leave college.* The important thing you need to know is who you are today and where you want to go next. Every experience you have will inform the next, and the best college choice begins with the best preparation.

We leave you with these poignant thoughts.

1. **Colleges look for reasons to accept—not reject—applicants.**
2. **Show them how you would enrich their community.**
3. **Seek your own truth!**

History tells us—and now science confirms—that students learn best in meaningful relationships with adults who care about them. For you to grow as a thinker and a productive member of society, you must have access to the multiple perspectives of other students, teachers, and mentors with different interests, aptitudes, and aspirations. Professor Andrew Delbanco at Columbia declares, "No outward mark of wealth or poverty can reveal the inward condition of the soul." In 1837 Ralph Waldo Emerson stated in his Phi Beta Kappa oration, "colleges gather various genius to their hospitable halls and set the hearts of their youth on flame." This desire to bring these diverse perspectives together for the pursuit of developing the individual is the hallmark of American higher education.

One brain, one discipline, will not be enough to solve the challenges you will face as you enter the global marketplace. College can prepare you to become the critical thinker and problem solver who will engage collectively and ask the probing questions —about what Delbanco expresses as "truth, justice, responsibility, and community"—that will move our civilization forward. American higher education seeks to shape the convictions of its students by stirring them to dig within themselves to find a meaningful life that goes beyond self-service to concern for others. This is the American college's gift to posterity. Guiding you to find your place in this spectrum of choices is our gift to you!

# YOUR FOUR-YEAR PLAN

We will leave you with a chart to map out your search to find your "U." In our extensive experience, we have determined that this systematic, thorough, and personal approach to the admission process provides students with the best fit in the college they ultimately attend.

Don't believe the hype. Although certain colleges may excel in certain arenas, there is no one college that is "the best" for every student. Finding the best "U" for you completely depends on how well you know yourself, your strengths, and your goals.

It's a big world out there, and there are many choices to make. Whenever the chatter of friends and their families who are also involved in the process overwhelms you, stop, take a deep breath, and go back to your plan.

Your official college record starts the moment you walk into high school. The choices you make at the beginning will shape the options you will have later. Make sure to focus on maintaining a strong academic record— sampling challenging courses as much as possible. Begin building an appropriate standardized testing profile. Assume leadership responsibilities. Use personal initiative to make a difference. Explore options for meaningful summer experiences. Develop a plan for visiting colleges.

We're in your corner. We know that if you keep your perspective and are true to yourself, whatever sweatshirt you end up wearing after your senior year will be one that fits you just right.

## FRESHMAN YEAR

### FIRST SEMESTER

| | |
|---|---|
| Get a social security number if you do not have one. | |
| Become involved in school activities. | |
| Begin keeping a log of your extracurricular activities at school and in your community, including quantifiable details. | |
| Work hard to keep up with the new demands of high school courses. | |
| While traveling during vacations, visit local college campuses to begin familiarizing yourself with college options. | |

### SECOND SEMESTER

| | |
|---|---|
| Start researching possible summer activities. | |
| Continue to stay involved in extracurricular activities, including volunteer work. | |
| Finalize plans for summer. | |
| Register for courses for sophomore year. | |

**Recommended Reading:**

*Lucky Fools* by Coert Voorhees

*Acceptance* by David Marcus

| SOPHOMORE YEAR | |
| --- | --- |
| **FIRST SEMESTER** | |
| Continue involvement in school activities, taking on greater responsibilities when possible. | |
| Keep up your log of extracurricular activities. | |
| Take the practice PSAT in October. | |
| Review results of your practice PSAT in December. | |
| Begin to evaluate your interests and skills. | |
| Continue visiting college campuses and researching websites. | |
| **SECOND SEMESTER** | |
| Start researching possible summer activities. | |
| Continue to stay involved in extracurricular activities, including volunteer work. | |
| Finalize plans for summer. | |
| Register for courses for junior year. | |
| Update your log of activities. | |
| Plan for summer prep for the upcoming fall PSAT. This is the official National Merit Qualifying Exam. | |

## Recommended Reading:

*Looking Beyond the Ivy League* by Loren Pope

*Colleges Unbound* by Jeffery Selingo

## JUNIOR YEAR

### FIRST SEMESTER

| | |
|---|---|
| Plan a family college discussion. | |
| Attend college fairs and information sessions. | |
| Create a file system to keep college information organized. | |
| Update your log of extracurricular activities, including quantifiable details. | |
| Take the PSAT in October at your school. | |
| Meet with college representatives visiting your school. | |
| Continue researching college websites. | |
| Begin learning the basics of financial aid. | |
| Build a personal relationship with your college counselor. | |
| Build relationships with several teachers who could be possible recommenders. | |
| Review PSAT results in December. | |
| Compose a list of questions to ask during college tours. | |
| Tour local campuses when visiting regions of the country. | |
| Register for standardized tests. | |
| Talk with college friends who are home on break. | |

| SECOND SEMESTER | |
|---|---|
| Prepare for the SAT and/or ACT. | |
| Start investigating summer opportunities. | |
| Continue making campus visits. | |
| Begin narrowing your college list. | |
| Keep up family college discussions. | |
| Estimate how much college will cost. | |
| Attend college fairs. | |
| Take SAT and/or ACT and any appropriate AP and/or Subject Tests. | |
| Finalize summer plans. | |
| Compare college requirements to course load. | |
| Select senior year courses. | |
| Determine who should write your letters of recommendation. | |
| Begin to think about content for your application essays over the summer. | |

## Recommended Reading:

*The Gatekeepers* by Jacque Steinber
*College Match* by Steven Antonoff

## SENIOR YEAR

### FIRST SEMESTER

| | |
|---|---|
| Retake standardized tests as necessary. | |
| Meet with high school counselor to finalize application plans and strategies. | |
| Decide whether or not to apply early action or early decision. | |
| Meet with college representatives visiting your school. | |
| Attend information sessions and college fairs. | |
| Fill out forms required by your high school office. | |
| Sign release forms so transcripts can be mailed to colleges. | |
| Report standardized test scores to colleges. | |
| Print a hard copy of each application as you submit. | |
| Be mindful of deadlines—create your own calendar. | |
| Arrange for college interviews, if appropriate. | |
| Submit early applications. | |
| Check College Portals regularly throughout your senior year. | |
| Prepare additional applications. | |
| Be vigilant about housing forms and deposits. | |

| SECOND SEMESTER | |
|---|---|
| Submit FAFSA as early as possible. Submit Individual College Profiles, if needed. | |
| Continue submitting regular decision applications. | |
| Maintain strong academic record. | |
| Expect notification of admission decisions no later than April 1st. | |
| Visit campuses you are considering attending, as needed. | |
| Compare financial aid packages. | |
| Sign and submit matriculation contract to one college by May 1st. | |
| Decline additional offers of admission. | |
| Submit roommate forms. | |
| Take any remaining achievement tests required. | |
| Write thank-you notes to those who supported you throughout the application process. | |
| Celebrate! | |

## Recommended Reading for Parents:

*Empty Nest—Full Heart: Journey from Home to College*
   by Andrea Van Steenhouse
*Letting Go: A Parent's Guide to the College Years*
   by Karen Coburn & Madge Treeger

# ABOUT THE
# AUTHORS

## JUDITH WIDENER MUIR – B.A., M.Ed., Ed.M., CEP

Judy Muir has worked with families and independent schools around the world for over thirty years. Managing expectations is a key component in serving students and their families. Muir's early training at the Gesell Institute of Child Development at Yale shaped the lens through which she views education, focusing on the process a child manifests in problem solving and skill building. A later degree as an Educational Diagnostician and Reading Specialist added clinical tools to her assessments of student progress.

As head of a Sacred Heart lower school for girls and then a school for children with learning differences, Muir empowered teachers to individualize instruction to meet the wide range of learners in their classrooms. She has designed curriculum for teachers and parents of children demonstrating exceptional potential for the Department of Education in Washington, D.C. She served for twelve years as the Associate Director of College Counseling at The Kinkaid School in Houston. She has also been the Director of a high-powered internship program at Kinkaid for the past twenty-eight years, placing over 130 seniors each January in three-week internship positions around the globe.

Muir is a graduate of The College of Wooster and holds a master's degree from the University of Houston. Muir also holds a graduate degree from Harvard University in Mind, Brain and Education and is a Teaching Fellow at Harvard's Graduate School of Education, where she commutes one day each week from Houston to help teach a class in Educational Neuroscience. She sits on the National Editorial Advisory Group for *The Fiske Guide to Colleges* and is a member of NACAC, TACAC, and a Professional Member of IECA.

## KATRIN MUIR LAU – B.A., M.A.

A s the daughter of a college counselor, Katrin Lau has been exploring college locations and the application process for decades. Family vacations provided an opportunity to visit yet another college campus along the way, and dinner conversations centered on the nuances of a campus or a college's decision to admit or deny. Lau's educational and professional journey has kept her focused on seeing beyond the obvious and communicating with poignant details. With a degree in Art History, she has worked at The National Gallery of Art in Washington, D.C. as well as Sotheby's Auction House in both Washington D.C. and New York City. She has also created an inter-disciplinary/project-based Art History curriculum and matched families to homes and antiques through Christie's international offerings. For the past four years she has used these skills in the arena of college counseling. As an artist, published photographer, art historian, and former varsity athlete, Mrs. Lau's counseling combines her expertise with a personal understanding of how students must craft their story to gain a seat at the college that will provide the best fit.

In her positions as College Counselor and Director of College Counseling at independent day schools, Lau has advised multiple international families, helping students navigate applications to England, Scotland, Canada, Germany, Spain, Norway, Singapore, Japan, and Australia – all with very different procedures. She also works with top athletic recruits, coordinating the efforts of students, parents, and coaches to navigate NCAA eligibility requirements and achieve their athletic aspirations.

A graduate of Southern Methodist University, Lau holds a master's degree from The University of Texas at Austin, plus a Graduate Certificate in the American Decorative Arts Program at Sotheby's, New York City. Additionally, she holds Certificates for further study of College Admission through the Harvard Summer Institute, The College Board, IECA Summer Training Program, and the University of California. She sits on the National Editorial Advisory Group for *The Fiske Guide to Colleges* and is a member of NACAC, TACAC, and a Professional Member of IECA.

*Judy Muir and Katrin Lau are based in Houston, Texas. Families from around the globe seek their direction in managing the complex college admission process that seems to lack transparency. Emerging high schools from around the world also call them to develop their college counseling programs – to hire and train staff, to develop the school's profile, to connect them to colleges; existing high schools seek them out to retool their programs and make them more effective in promoting personal growth.*

*Watch their website for timely details to stay on track, wherever you are in the frenetic process of finding your U during the flurry of finding your University. They can help you make the elusive process manageable, keep you steady, and help you emerge with your relationships intact.*

Let us help you find your U.

**www.educationalplan.com**

judy@educationalplan.com
katrin@educationalplan.com

# AFTERWORD

## Reply to W.M.B
## or
## *Gee, We Really Loved Your Poem*

We are addressed by petitions
Here in the Office of Rice Admission:

We get a deluge of applications,
All with impressive recommendations;

We get respectful encomiums from preachers,
Thousands of letters from counselors and teachers;

Sheaves of transcripts from each registrar,
Millions of calls from near and far;

Inquiries from applicants in anguished modes,
But we almost never receive any Odes.

We're seldom honored by couplet and wit,
And we loved all of it—every bit!

Rarely have we an engineer-versifier
Seeking our great education that's higher.

So here's our verse to you, W.M.B.,
Hilarious with your metric plea:

Such a poet shall not be "Wait-Listed" thrice,
We joyously offer you admission to Rice.

Reproduced with permission from Richard M. Stabell
Dean of Admission Emeritus
Rice University

# ENDNOTES

We looked at the new science of epigenetics for clues about engaging teens more effectively in the runaway college application process. Research about sleep debt (we know our teens are not getting enough sleep!), the impact of stress (the hallmark of the college admission process!) on teens' long-term health, motivation (how to keep teens engaged in a seemingly amorphous process in which they perceive they lack any control over outcome!), and new research on how students learn best (the driver for finding their best college fit!) made us rethink the approaches we might use with the families who come to us full of angst, seeking clarity and direction.

We have included both the books and authors that have informed our work, as well as the studies and scholars that have moved us from reasonable hypothesis to information grounded in empirical data about timely issues regarding teen brain development and family dynamics in the digital world we now inhabit.

While our text attempts to distill the college application process itself, we want to share pivotal research about teen development plus poignant concepts about the current educational challenges the colleges are facing, as well. Our readers who want to dig deeper and understand better can use a combination of the text, these notes, and the reference list.

International families seek our counsel regularly, perplexed about how the American higher educational system works. They find the "holistic" review process particularly mysterious. Alas, so do our American families! Confusion crosses demographic and cultural lines equally. We seek to demystify the process. We hope our guide will help you find the process more manageable and keep your relationships less stressful—that our research can help you, too, share the sense of awe we feel for the teens with whom we work!

## CHAPTER: A Message About Our Purpose

Clayton Christensen – Professor of Business Administration at Harvard Business School, raises alarms about how escalating debt and current technology are threatening the model that has defined higher education for hundreds of years. He looks at changing demands on universities as they seek to balance their budgets and meet the expectations of incoming students by identifying what students they serve, what subjects they emphasize, what types of scholarship they pursue.

Christensen, C., Eyring, H. (2011). The innovative university: Changing the DNA of higher education. San Francisco, CA: Jossey-Bass. p. 27.

*an increasingly complex process:* We dug into Jeffrey Selingo's College (un) Bound as a credible and thought-provoking voice in the issues reflected in this opening chapter about the complexity of the process, the value of a traditional college education, and the challenges colleges face for sustainability. Selingo, J. (2013). College (un) bound: The future of higher education and what it means for students. New York: Houghton Mifflin Harcourt. pp. 19-34.

*empirical research focusing on teen brain development:* the following research, in particular, grounded the message in the opening chapters.

National Scientific Council on the Developing Child (2004). *Children's emotional development is built into the architecture of their brains.* Working Paper No. 2.

National Scientific Council on the Developing Child (2010). *Early experiences can alter gene expression and affect long-term development.* Working Paper No. 10.

National Scientific Council on the Developing Child. (2007). *The Science of Early Childhood Development: Closing the Gap Between What We Know and What We Do.* http://developingchild.harvard.edu/library/

reports_and_working_papers/science_of_early_childhood_development/

National Scientific Council on the Developing Child. (2008). *The timing and quality of early experiences combine to shape brain architecture.* Working Paper No.5

National Scientific Council on the Developing Child. (2010). *Persistent fear and anxiety can affect young children's learning and development.* Working Paper No. 9. http://developingchild.harvard.edu/library/reports_and_working_papers/working_papers/wp9/

*the process is rapidly changing:* Selingo identifies the change agents and how media is becoming a strong arm in college admission. Selingo, J. (2013). College (un) bound: The future of higher education and what it means for students. New York: Houghton Mifflin Harcourt. pp. 19-34.

*Much of what we have done until recently simply does not make sense any more in the digital landscape:* references about the hours students are engaging with media are from the findings of Jane McGonigal and her surprising accounts of what we are learning about the media, a worthy read. McGonigal, J. (2011). Reality is broken: Why games make us better and how they can change the world. New York: The Penguin Press. pp. 1-354.

*challenge families to rethink pathways to succeed:* the return on investment for college dollars is challenged by families that share a concern about their graduates getting jobs after graduation. Selingo, J. (2013). College (un) bound: The future of higher education and what it means for students. New York: Houghton Mifflin Harcourt. pp. 160-170.

*the stress response system kicks in:* stress is the hallmark of the college application process where teens feel they have little to no control over outcome.

McEwen, B., and Lasley, E. (2002). The end of stress as we know it. New York: Dana Press. pp. 1-202.

McEwen, B. (2008). Central effects of stress hormones in health and disease: Understanding the protective and damaging effects of stress and stress mediators. *European Journal of Pharmacology,* 583, pp. 174-185.

National Scientific Council on the Developing Child (2005). *Excessive stress disrupts the architecture of the developing brain.* Working Paper No. 3.

------------------------------------

## CHAPTER: Why American Higher Education Is Unique

Derek Bok – former President of Harvard, William Bowen – former President of Princeton, Andrew Delbanco – Professor of Humanities at Columbia, and Mark Edmundson – Professor at The University of Virginia are among the scholars who gain our rapt attention about the importance of preserving the liberal arts college programs. Each addresses the needs of our democracy, which must have discerning voters to flourish, and our economic pipeline, which requires a continuing supply of trained workers to sustain. Trends reveal exploding costs and expanding online learning opportunities. The debate heats up. These scholars form the basis for this chapter.

Bok, D. (2013). Higher education in america. Princeton: Princeton University Press. pp. 1-412.

Bowen, W. (2013). Higher education in the digital age. Princeton, NJ: University Press. pp. 1-161.

Delbanco, A. (2012). College: What it was, is, and should be. Princeton: Princeton University Press. pp. 1-177.

Edmundson, M. (2013). Why teach: In defense of a real education. New York: Bloomsbury USA. pp. vii – 222.

Andrew Delbanco makes a compelling case for the value of a liberal arts education, citing eloquently how the best thoughts of the past will serve the future well:

*transmits knowledge of and from the past:* Delbanco, A. (2012). College: What it was, is, and should be. Princeton: Princeton University Press. p. 2.

*new knowledge in order to supersede the past:* Delbanco, A. (2012). College: What it was, is, and should be. Princeton: Princeton University Press. p. 2.

*cutting edge research in both:* Delbanco, A. (2012). College: What it was, is, and should be. Princeton: Princeton University Press. p. 3.

*perhaps the most fundamental value:* Pace, E. (1988). *Kingman Brewster Jr., 69, Ex-Yale President and U.S. Envoy, Dies. New York Times.* Archived, November 9. (http://www.nytimes.com/1988/11/09/obituaries/kingman-brewster-jr-69-ex-yale-president-and-us-envoy-dies.html)

*widespread debate over what you should be learning...and what you'll need to know:*

Christensen, C., Eyring, H. (2011). The innovative university: Changing the DNA of higher education. San Francisco, CA: Jossey-Bass. p. 27.

*where there is a single right answer...we have not found any...alternatives to expert human teachers...:* Delbanco, A. (2012). College: What it was, is, and should be. Princeton: Princeton University Press. p. 5.

------------------------------------

## CHAPTER: Why The Admission Process Is So Complex

*recent economic turbulence:* Christensen, C., Eyring, H. (2011). The innovative university: Changing the DNA of higher education. San Francisco, CA: Jossey-Bass. p. 7.

*science confirms that students learn best in meaningful relationships:* National Scientific Council on the Developing Child. (2004). *Young children develop in an environment of relationships.* Working Paper No.1. *multiple perspectives...are essential for each student to grow:* Edmundson, M. (2013).

Why teach: In defense of a real education. New York: Bloomsbury USA. p. 45.

*no outward mark of wealth or poverty can reveal the inward condition of the soul:* Delbanco, A. (2012). College: What it was, is, and should be. Princeton: Princeton University Press. p. 171.

*colleges gather various genius to their hospitable halls…:* Emerson, R. (1837) as quoted in Delbanco, A. (2012). College: What it was, is, and should be. Princeton: Princeton University Press. p. 172.

*truth, justice, responsibility:* Delbanco, A. (2012). College: What it was, is, and should be. Princeton: Princeton University Press. p. 173.

*stirring them to dig deep within themselves:* Edmundson, M. (2013). Why teach: In defense of a real education. New York: Bloomsbury USA. p. 46.

*beyond self-service:* Delbanco, A. (2012). College: What it was, is, and should be. Princeton: Princeton University Press. p. 177

# REFERENCES

## COLLEGE RESOURCES

Antonoff, S. (2011). The college finder: Choose the school that's right for you. Westford, MA: Wintergreen Orchard House.

Antonoff, S. (2014). College Match: A blueprint for choosing the best school for you. EDUconsultingMedia.com. pp. 1-172.

Coburn, K. & Treeger, M. (2003). Letting go: A parent's guide to understanding the college years. New York: HarperCollins. pp 3-411.

CollegeBoard. (2014). International Student Handbook. New York: The College Board. pp. 4-44.

Fiske, E. (2015). Fiske guide to colleges. Naperville, IL: Sourcebooks.

Fiske, E. & Hammond, B. (2010). Fiske guide to getting into the right college. Naperville, IL: Sourcebooks. pp. 3-334.

Fiske, E. & Hammond, B. (2011). Real college essays that work. Naperville, IL: Sourcebooks. pp. 3-338.

Marcus, D. (2010). Acceptance: A legendary guidance counselor helps seven kids find the right colleges – and find themselves. New York: Penguin. pp. 1-272.

Pope, L. (2012). Colleges that change lives: 40 schools that will change the way you think about colleges. New York: Penguin Group. pp. 1-352.

Pope, L. (2007). Looking beyond the ivy league: finding the college that's right for you. New York: Penguin Group. pp. 1-288.

Soares, J. (2012). Sat wars: The case for test-optional college admissions New York: Teachers College Press. pp. 1-211.

Steenhouse, A. (2002). Empty nest...full heart: The journey from home to college. Denver: Simpler Life Press. pp. 1-188.

Steinberg, J. (2002). The gate-keepers: Inside the admissions process of a premier college. New York: Penguin. pp. 1-284.

Voorhees, C. (2012). Lucky Fools. New York: Hyperion. pp. 1-293.

Woodacre, M. & Bane, S. (2006). I'll miss you too: An off-to-college guide for parents and students – what will change, what will not, and how we'll stay connected. Naperville, IL: Sourcebooks. pp. 1-204.

## TRENDS IN AMERICAN HIGHER EDUCATION, BOOKS

Abelson, H., Ledeen, K., & Lewis, H. (2008). Blown to bits: Your life, liberty, and happiness after the digital explosion. Boston: Addison-Wesley. pp. 1-316.

Anderson, C. (2012). Makers: The new industrial revolution. New York: Random House. pp. 3-229.

Bok, D. (2013). Higher education in america. Princeton: Princeton University Press. pp. 1-412.

Bowen, W. (2013). Higher education in the digital age. Princeton, NJ: University Press. pp. 1-161.

Christensen, C., Eyring, H. (2011). The innovative university: Changing the DNA of higher education. San Francisco, CA: Jossey-Bass. pp. 3-401.

Christensen, C., Horn, M. & Johnson, C. (2008). Disrupting class: How disruptive innovation will change the way the world learns. New York: McGraw Hill. pp. 1-230.

Delbanco, A. (2012). College: What it was, is, and should be. Princeton: Princeton University Press. pp. 1-177.

Edmundson, M. (2013). Why teach: In defense of a real education. New York: Bloomsbury USA. pp. vii – 222.

Hatch, M. (2014). The maker movement manifesto: Rules for innovation in the new world of crafters, hackers, and tinkerers. New York: McGraw-Hill. pp. 1-204.

Kahneman, D. (2011). Thinking, fast and slow. New York: Farrar, Straus and Giroux. pp. 3-446.

Selingo, J. (2013). College (un) bound: The future of higher education and what it means for students. New York: Houghton Mifflin Harcourt. pp. 3-212.

Zhao, Yong. (2009). Catching up or leading the way: American education in the age of globalization. Alexandria, VA: ASCD. pp. 1-202.

Zhao, Yong. (2012). World class leaders: Educating creative and entrepreneurial students. Thousand Oaks, CA: Corwin. pp. 1-256.

## HOW THE INFORMATION EXPLOSION IS CHANGING PARENTING

Brazelton, B. and Greenspan, S. (2000). The irreducible needs of children: What every child must have to grow, learn, and flourish. Cambridge, MA: Perseus Books. pp. 1-201.

Brooks, R. and Goldstein, S. (2003). Nurturing resilience in our children: Answers to the most important parenting questions. New York: McGraw Hill. pp. 1-234.

Buonomano, D. (2011). Brain bugs: How the brain's flaws shape our lives. New York: WW Norton & Company, Inc. pp. 1-235.

Christensen, C., Allworth, J. & Dillon, K. (2012). How will you measure your life? New York: HarperCollins. pp. 1-221.

Dobbs, D. (2009). Orchid children. *The Atlantic December*. pp.60-68. http://www.theatlantic.com/doc/200912/dobbs-orchid-gene

Dweck, C. (2006). Mindset: The new psychology of success. New York: Random House. pp. 1-239.

Eagleman, D. (2011). Incognito: The secret lives of the brain. New York: Pantheon Books. pp. 1-225.

Elkind, D. (1984). All grown up and no place to go: Teenagers in crisis. Reading, MA: Addison-Wesley. pp. 1-216.

Elkind, D. (2007). The power of play: How spontaneous imaginative activities lead to happier, healthier children. Cambridge, MA: Perseus. pp. 1-218.

Gardner, H. (2004). Changing minds: The art and science of changing our own and other people's minds. Boston: Harvard Business School Press.

Gardner, H. (2000). The disciplined mind: Beyond facts standardized tests K 12 education that every child deserves, Penguin Group.

Gardner, H. (2006). Five minds for the future. Cambridge: Harvard Business School Press.

Gardner, H. (2004). The unschooled mind: How children think and how schools should teach, Basic Books.

Gardner, H., Csikzentmihalyi, M., and Damon, W. (2001). Good work: When excellence and ethics meet. New York: Basic Books.

Gee, J. (2007). What video games have to teach us about learning and literacy. New York: Palgrave Macmillan. pp. 1-212.

Gopnik, A., Meltzoff, A. & Kuhl, P. (1999). The scientist in the crib: What early learning tells us about the mind. New York: HarperCollins.

Gopnik, A. (2012). What's wrong with the teenage mind? *Wall Street Journal*. January 28, Section C, p. 1.

Hallowell, E. (2006). Crazy Busy: Overstretched, overbooked, and about to snap. New York: Ballantine Books. pp. 1-229.

Hallowell, E. (1997). Worry: Controlling it and using it wisely. New York: Pantheon Books. pp. 1-306

Ilg, F., Ames, L. & Baker, S. (1981). Child Behavior: The classic child care manual from the Gesell Institute of Human Development. New York: HarperCollins. pp. 1-347.

Kegan, R. & Lahey, L. (2001). How the way we talk can change the way we work. San Francisco, CA: Jossey-Bass. pp. 1-227.

Kegan, R. & Lahey, L. (2009). Immunity to change: How to overcome it and unlock the potential in yourself and your organization. Boston: Harvard Business Press. pp. 1-64.

Kohn, A. (2005). Unconditional parenting: Moving from rewards and punishments to love and reason. New York: Atria Books.

McEwen, B., and Lasley, E. (2002). The end of stress as we know it. New York: Dana Press. pp. 1-202.

McEwen, B. (2008). Central effects of stress hormones in health and disease: Understanding the protective and damaging effects of stress and stress mediators. *European Journal of Pharmacology*, 583, pp. 174-185.

McGonigal, J. (2011). Reality is broken: Why games make us better and how they can change the world. New York: The Penguin Press. pp. 1-354.

Medina, J. (2008). Brain rules. Seattle, WA: Pear Press. pp. 1-280.

Mele, N. (2013). The end of big: How the internet makes david the new goliath. New York: St. Martin's Press. pp. 1-270.

Muir, J. (2012). Live wires: Neuro-parenting to ignite your teen's brain. Houston: Bright Sky Press. pp. 10-160.

Mukunda, G. (2012). Indispensable: When leaders really matter. Boston: Harvard Business School Publishing. pp. 1-249.

Nisbett, R. (2009). Intelligence and how to get it: Why schools and cultures count. New York: W. W. Norton & Company. pp. 1-235.

Nodelman, P. and Reimer, M. (2003). The pleasures of children's literature. Boston: Allyn and Bacon. pp. 1-329.

Nye, J. (2013). Presidential leadership and the creation of the American era. Princeton: Princeton University Press. pp. 1-159.

Pennebaker, J. (2011). The secret life of pronouns: What our words say about us. New York: Bloomsbury Press. pp. 1-299.

Prensky, M. (2000). Digital game-based learning. New York: McGraw-Hill.

Prensky, M. (2006). Don't bother me, mom: I'm learning. New York: Paragon.

Ratey, J. (2001). A user's guide to the brain. New York: Pantheon Books. pp. 1-378.

Ratey, J. and Hagerman, E. (2008). Spark: The revolutionary new science of exercise and the brain. New York: Little Brown and Company. pp. 1-268.

Restak, R. (2002). The secret life of the brain. New York: Pantheon Books.

Restak, R. (2003). The new brain: How the modern age is rewiring your mind. New York: Rodale Press.

Sandel, M. (2012). What money can't buy: The moral limits of markets. New York: Farrar, Straus & Giroux. pp. 3-203.

Sapolsky, R. (2004). Why zebras don't have ulcers: An updated guide to stress, stress related diseases, and coping (3rd ed.). New York: Owl Books.

Seligman, M. with Reivich, K., Jaycox, L. and Gillham, J. (1995). The optimistic child: A proven program to safeguard children against depression and build lifelong resilience. New York: Houghton Mifflin. pp. 1-305.

Schwartz, T. (2010). Be excellent at anything: The four keys to transforming the way we work and live. NY: Free Press. pp. 1-275.

Shonkoff, J. and Phillips, D. (Eds.). 2000. *From neurons to neighborhoods: The Science of early childhood development.* National Research Council and Institute of Medicine. Washington, D.C.: National Academy Press. pp. 1-413.

Silvey, A. (Ed.). (2002). The essential guide to children's books and their creators. New York: Houghton Mifflin. pp. 1-498.

Simpson, A. Rae. (2001). Raising teens: A synthesis of research and a foundation for action. Boston: Center for Health Communication, Harvard School of Public Health. pp. 1-68.

Spooner, J. (2012). No one ever told us that: Money and life, letters to my grandchildren. New York: Hatchette Book Group. pp. 1-231.

Steiner-adair, C. (2013). The big disconnect: Protecting childhood and family relationships in the digital age. New York: HarperCollins. pp. 1-295.

Strauch, B. (2003). The Primal Teen: What the new discoveries about the teenage brain tell us about our kids. New York: Random House. pp. 3-220.

Thompson, C. (2013). Smarter than you think: How technology is changing our minds for the better. New York: Penguin Press. pp. 1-288.

Wagner, T. (2012). Creating Innovators: The making of young people who will change the world. New York: Scribner. pp. 1-251.

Weissbourd, R. (2009). The parents we mean to be: How well-intentioned adults undermine children's moral and emotional development. New York: Houghton Mifflin Harcourt Brace Publishing. pp. 1-206.

Wheelan, C. (2013). Naked statistics: Stripping the dread from the data. New York: W. W. Norton. pp. 1-260.

Wolf, M. (2007). Proust and the squid: The story and science of the reading brain. New York: HarperCollins Publishers. pp. 1-236.

## BRAIN DEVELOPMENT, RESEARCH STUDIES

Achtman, R. L., Green, C. S., & Bavelier, D. (2008). Video games as a tool to train visual skills. *Restorative neurology and neuroscience*, 26(4), 435–446.

Adachi, P. J. C., & Willoughby, T. (2013). Do Video Games Promote Positive Youth D Alloway, T. (2006). How does working memory work in the classroom? *Educational Research and Reviews*, 1(4). pp. 134-149. evelopment? *Journal of Adolescent Research*, 28(2), 155–165.

Anderson, D. (2004). Watching children watch television and the creation of *blue's clues*. In H. Hendershot (Ed.). *Nickelodeon nation: The history, politics, and economics of America's only TV channel for kids*. New York: New York University Press.

Anderson, M. L. (2010). Neural reuse: A fundamental organizational principle of the brain. Behavioral and brain sciences, 33, 245-313.

Annetta, L. A., Minogue, J., Holmes, S. Y., & Cheng, M.-T. (2009). Computers & Education. *Computers & Education*, 53(1), 74–85.

Ansary, N. A.. & Luthar, S. S. (2009). Distress and academic achievement among adolescents of affluence: A study of externalizing and internalizing problem behaviors and school performance. Development and Psychopathology, 21, 319-341.

Asch, S. E. (1948). The doctrine of suggestion, prestige and imitation in social psychology. ''Psychological Review'', 55, 250–276.

Baddeley, A. (2003). Working memory: Looking back and looking forward. Nature Reviews, 4, 829-839.

Bandura, A. (2001). Social cognitive theory of mass communication. *Media Psychology, 3*. pp. 265-299.

Banich, M. (2004). Cognitive neuroschience and neuropsychology. Boston: Houghton Mifflin. pp. 3-61 and 285-428.

Barker, D., Osmond, C., Forsen, T., Kajantie, E., & Erikson, J. (2005). Trajectories of growth among children who have coronary events as adults. *The New England Journal of Medicine, 353,* 1802-1809.

Barkley, R. (1997). Behavioral inhibition, sustained attention and executive functions: Constructing a unifying theory of ADHD.Psychological Bulletin, 121(1), 65-94.

Barlett, C. P., Barlett, C. P., Vowels, C. L., Vowels, C. L., Shanteau, J., Shanteau, J., et al. (2009). The effect of violent and non-violent computer games on cognitive performance. *Computers in Human Behavior*, 25(1), 96–102.

Bartholow, B. D., Bushman, B. J., & Sestir, M. A. (2006). Chronic violent video game exposure and desensitization to violence: Behavioral and event-related brain potential data. *Journal of Experimental Social Psychology, 42*(4), 532–539.

Bavelier, D., Green, C. S., Pouget, A., & Schrater, P. (2012). Brain Plasticity Through the Life Span: Learning to Learn and Action Video Games. *Annual Review of Neuroscience, 35*(1), 391–416.

Becker, B., & Luthar S. S. (2007). Peer-perceived admiration and social preference: contextual correlates of positive peer regard among suburban and urban adolescents. Journal of research on adolescence, 17(1), 117-144.

Belchior, P. C., Marsiske, M., Sisco, S. M., Yam, A., Bavelier, D., Ball, K., & Mann, W. C. (2013). Computers in Human Behavior. *Computers in Human Behavior, 29*(4), 1318–1324.

Blakemore, S. J., Burnett, S., & Dahl, R. E. (2010). The role of puberty in the developing adolescent brain. Human Brain Mapping, 31, 926-933. (DOI: 10.1002/hbm.21052).

Blakemore, S., den Ouden, H., Choudhury, S., & Frith, C. (2007). Adolescent development of the nerual circuitry for thinking about intentions. *SCAN, 2.* pp. 130-139.

Bronfenbrenner, U. (1979). *The ecology of human development: Experiments by nature and design.* Cambridge: Harvard University Press. pp. 3-42.

Bushman, B. and Huesmann, L. (2001). Effects of televised violence on aggression. Chapter 11 in Singer and Singer.

Cahill, L., McGaugh, J. L., & Weinberger, N. M. (2001). The neurobiology of learning and memory: some reminders to remember. Trends in Neurosciences, 24, 10, 578-581.

Cameron, J., & Pierce, W. (1994). Reinforcement, reward, and intrinsic motivation: A meta-analysis. Review of Educational Research, 64, 3, 363-423.

Cameron, J., Banko, K., & Pierce, W. (2001). Pervasive negative effects of rewards on intrinsic motivation: The myth continues. The Behavior Analyst, 24, 1-44.

Cassidy, J. & Shaver, P. (Eds.) (1999). Handbook of Attachment: Theory, research, and clinical applications. New York: Guilford. pp. 89-111.

Cattell, R.B. (1963). Theory of fluid and crystallized intelligence: A critical experiment. Journal of Educational Psychology, 54, 1-22.

Champ, J. (2004). "Couch potatodom" reconsidered: The vogels and the carsons. In S. M. Hoover, L. S. Clark, and D. F. Alters. *Media, home and family.* New York and London: Routledge.

Chen, L., Baker, S., Braver, E., & Guohua, L. (2000). Carrying passengers as a risk factor for crashes fatal to 16-17 year old drivers. *Journal of the American Medical Assoication, 283*(12). pp.1578-1582.

Cohn, L., Macfarlane, S., & Yanez, C. (1995). Risk-perception: Differences between adolescents and adults. *Health Psychology, 14*(3). pp. 217-222.

Collins, F. (2010). Genetics loads the gun and environment pulls the trigger. http://blog.pathway.com/genetics-loads-the-gun-and-environment-pulls-the-trigger-dr-francis-collins/.

Collins, J. (2001). Good to great: Why some companies make the leap…and others don't. New York: Harper Collins. pp. 1-258.

Csikszentmihalyi, M. (1990). Flow: The psychology of optimal experience. New York: HarperCollins.

Damasio, A. (2003). Looking for Spinoza: Joy, sorrow, and the feeling brain. New York: Harcourt.

Damasio, A. (1999). The feeling of what happens: Body and emotion in the making of consciousness. New York: Harcourt.

Danese, A., Moffitt, T., Harrington, H., Milne, B., Polanczyk, G., Pariante, C., Poulton, R., & Caspi, A. (2009). Adverse childhood experiences and adult risk factors for age-related disease. *Archives of Pediatrics and Adolescent Medicine, 163*, 1135-1143.

Davies, G., Tenesa, A., Payton, A., Yang, J., Harris, S.E. et al. (2011). Genome-wide association studies establish that human intelligence is highly heritable and polygenetic. Molecular psychiatry, 16, 996-1005.

Deary, I. J., Penke, L., & Johnson, W. (2010). The neuroscience of human intelligence differences. Nature reviews neuroscience, 11, 201-211.

Deary, I. J., Strand, S., Smith, P. & Fernandes, C. (2007). Intelligence and educational achievement. Intelligence, 35, 13-21.

Deci, E., Koestner, R., Ryan, R. (1999). A meta-analytic review of experiments examining the effects of extrinsic rewards on intrinsic motivation. Psychological Bulletin, 125, 627-668.

Deci, E., Vallerand, R. Pelletier, L., & Ryan, R. (1991). Motivation and education: The self-determination perspective. *Educational Psychologist, 26*(3/4). pp. 325-346.

Dietrich, C. (2010). Decision making: Factors that influence decision making, heuristics used, and decision outcomes. *Student Pulse,* 2.02. Retrieved from: http://www.studentpulse.com/a?id=180.

Dweck, C. (2002). The development of ability conceptions. In A. Wigfield & J.S. Eccles (Eds.), *Development of achievement motivation.* San Diego, CA: Academic Press. pp. 57-88.

Dye, M. W., Green, C. S., & Bavelier, D. (2009). Increasing speed of processing with action video games. *Current Directions in Psychological Science, 18*(6), 321–326.

Engle, P., Black, M., Behrman, J., Cabral de Mello, M., Gertler, P., Kapiriri, L., Martorell, R., Young, M., & the International Child Development Steering Group. (2007). Strategies to avoid the loss of developmental potential in more than 200 million children in the developing world. *Lancet, 369,* 229-242.

Evans, G. W., & Schamberg, M. A. (2009). Childhood poverty, chronic stress, and adult working memory. Proceedings of the National Academy of Science, 106(16): 6545-6549.

Farah, M.J., Illes, J., Cook-Deegan, R., Gardner, H., Kandel, E., King, P., Parens, E., Sahakian, B., & Wolpe, P.R. (2004). Neurocognitive enhancement: What can we do and what should we do? Nature Reviews, 5, 421-425.

Fisch, S. M., R. T. Truglio, and C. F. Cole (1999). The impact of *Sesame Street* on preschool children: A review and synthesis of 30 years' research. *Media Psychology, 1,* 165-190.

Fischer, K. (2009). Mind, Brain, and Education: Building a scientific groundwork for learning and teaching. *Mind, Brain, and Education, 3.* pp. 2-15.

Fischer, K. and Immordino-Yang, M. (2008). The fundamental importance of the brain and learning for education. *The Jossey-Bass Reader on the Brain and Learning.* San Francisco: Jossey-Bass. xvii-xxi.

Fischer, K., Bernstein, J. & Immordino-Yang, M. (Eds.). (2007). Mind, brain, and education in reading disorders. Cambridge UK: University Press. pp. 181-238.

Fischer, K, Ayoub, C., Noam, G., Singh, I., Maraganore, A., & Raya, J. (1997). Psychopathology as adaptive development along distinctive pathways. *Development and Psychopathology, 9.* pp. 751-781.

Gabrieli, J. (1998). Cognitive neuroscience of human memory. Annual Review of Psychology, 49, 87-115.

Galvan, A. (2010). Neural plasticity of development and learning. *Human Brain Mapping,* 31. pp. 879-890.

Goldberg, S. (1991). Recent developments in attachment theory and research. *Canadian Journal of Psychiatry,* 36. pp. 393-400.

Goldin, C. & Katz, L.F. (2007). The race between education and technology: The evolution of U.S. educational wage differentials, 1890 to 2005. Working Paper No. 12984, National Bureau of Economic Research. (http://www.nber.org/papers/w12984).

Gormley, W. (2007). Early childhood care and education: Lessons and puzzles. *Journal of Policy Analysis and Management, 26,* 633-671.

Gould, S. (1996). The mismeasure of man. New York: Norton. pp. 176-263.

Gray, H. (1995). It's a different world where you come from. Chapter 6 in *Watching race: Television and the struggle for "blackness."* Minneapolis: University of Minnesota Press.

Griffin, S., Case, R., Siegler, R. (1994). Rightstart: Providing the central conceptual prerequisites for the first formal learning of arithmetic to students at risk for school failure. In K. McGilly (Ed.), *Classroom lessons: Integrating cognitive theory and classroom practice.* Cambridge, MA: MIT Press. pp. 25-49.

Gunderson, L., & Siegel, L.S. (2001). The evils of the use of IQ tests to define learning disabilities in first- and second- language learners. The Reading Teacher, 55(1), 48-55.

Gunnar, M. & Davis, E. (2003). Stress and emotion in early childhood. In R.M. Lerner & M.A. Easterbrooks (Eds.), Handbook of Psychology, Vol. 6. Developmental Psychology. New York: Wiley. pp. 113-134.

Hammond, L. D., Austin, K., & Rosso, J. (2001). How people learn: Introduction to learning theories.

Harris, P. (2007, September 18). Attachment and the effects of early deprivation. [H-250 Lecture, HGSE]. Cambridge, MA.

Harris, P. (2007, October 30). Emotions and understanding emotions. [H-250 Lecture, HGSE]. Cambridge, MA.

Harris, P. (2007, November 1). Emotion and understanding emotions. [H-250 Lecture, HGSE]. Cambridge, MA.

Harris, P. (1989). *Children and emotion.* Malden, MA: Blackwell Publishers. pp 1-215.

Harris, P. (in press). Understanding emotion. To appear in M. Lewis & J. M. Haviland-Jones (Eds.) Handbook of Emotions 3rd edition. New York: Guilford Press.

Hart, B. and Risley, T. (1992). American Parenting of Language-Learning Children: Persisting Differences in Family-Child Interactions Observed in Natural Home Environments, *Developmental Psychology,* Vol. 28, No. 6, 1096-1105.

Hattie, J., & Timperley, H. (2007). The power of feedback. Review of Educational Research, 77, 1, 81-112.

Heckman, J., & Masterov, D. (2007). The productivity argument for investing in young children. T.W. Shultz Award Lecture presented to the Allied Social Sciences Association. *Review of Agricultural Economics, 29,* 446-493.

Hinton, C. and Fischer, K. (2008). Research schools: Grounding research I educational practice. *Mind, Brain, and Education, 2.* pp. 157-160.

Huesmann, L. (2007). The impact of electronic media violence: Scientific theory and research. *Journal of Adolescent Health,* vol 41, 6, supplement 1.

Hofschire, L. and Greenberg, B. (2002). Media's impact on adolescents' body dissatisfaction. In J. D. Brown, J. R. Steele, and K. Walsh-Childers (Eds.). *Sexual teens, sexual media: Investigating media's influence on adolescent sexuality.* Mahwah, NJ: Lawrence Erlbaum Associates.

Horning, K. (1997). From cover to cover: Evaluating and reviewing children's books. NY: Harper Collins. pp. 1-220.

Hubert-Wallander, B., Green, S. C., & Bavelier, D. (2010). Stretching the limits of visual attention: the case of action video games. *WIREs Cognitive Science*, Wiley, 1, 1-9.

Immordino-Yang, M., McColl, A., Damasio, A. & Damasio, H. (2009). Neural correlates of admiration and compassion. *Proceedings of the national academy of sciences*, 106(19). pp. 8021-8026.

Jordan, A. (1996). *The state of children's television: An examination of quantity, quality, and industry beliefs.* Philadelphia: The Annenberg Public Policy Center of the University of Pennsylvania.

Kishiyama, M., Boyce, W.T., Jimenez, A., Perry, L., & Knight, R. (2009). Socioeconomic disparities affect prefrontal function in children. *Journal of Cognitive Neuroscience, 21*, 1106-1115.

Knudsen, E., Heckman, J., Cameron, J., & Shonkoff, J. (2006). Economic, neurobiological and behavioral perspectives on building america's future workforce. *Proceedings of the National Academy of Sciences, 103*. pp. 10155-10162.

Knudsen, E. (2004). Sensitive periods in the development of the brain and behavior. *Journal of Cognitive Neuroscience, 16.* pp. 1412-1425.

Kruger, J., & Dunning, D. (1999). Unskilled and unaware of it: How difficulties in recognizing one's own incompetence lead to inflated self-assessments. *Journal of Personality and Social Psychology*, 77, 6, 1121-1134.

Kunkel, D. (2001). Children and television advertising. Chapter 19 in Singer and Singer.

Lamb, S., and L. M. Brown (2007). See no evil? What girls watch. Chapter 2 in *Packaging girlhood: Rescuing our daughters from marketers' schemes.* New York: St. Martin's Griffin.

LeDoux, J. (2000). Emotion circuits in the brain. Annual Review of Neuroscience, 23,. pp. 155-184.

LeDoux, J. (1996). The emotional brain. NY: Simon & Schuster.

LeDoux, J. (2002). Synaptic self: How our brains become who we are. NY: Penguin.

Livingstone, S. (2002). Living together separately: The family context of media use. Chapter 5 in *Young people and new media: Childhood and the changing media environment.* Thousand Oaks, CA: Sage Publications.

Loehr, J., and Schwartz, T. (2010). The power of full engagement: Managing energy, not time, is the key to high performance and personal renewal. New York: Simon and Schuster. pp. 1-195.

Luthar, S. S. (2006). "Overscheduling" versus other stressors: Challenges of high socioeconomic status families.Social Policy Report, Society for Research in Child Development.

Luthar, S. S., Shoum, K. A.,Brown, P.J. (2006). Extracurricular involvement among affluent youth: A scapegoat for "ubiquitous achievement pressures"?. Developmental Psychology, 42, 583-597.

Luthar, S. S., & Latendresse, S. J. (2005). Children of the affluent: Challenges to well-being. Current Directions in Psychological Science,14 , 49-53.

Luthar, S. S., & Sexton, C. (2005). The high price of affluence. In R. V. Kail (Ed.), Advances in Child Development, 32, 126-162. San Diego, CA: Academic Press.

Luthar, S. S. (2003). The culture of affluence: Psychological costs of material wealth.Child Development, 74, 1581-1593.

Lynch, M.A. (2004). Long-term potentiation and memory. Physiology Review, 84, 88-136.

Mares, M. and Woodard, E. (2001). Prosocial effects on children's social interactions. Chapter 9 in Singer and Singer.

Meaney, M. (2010). Epigenetics and the biological definition of gene x environment interactions. *Child Development, 81*, 41-79.

Milner, B., Squire, L., & Kandel, E. (1998). Cognitive neuroscience and the study of memory. Neuron, 20, 445-468.

Mischel, W., Shoda, Y., & Rodriguez, M. (1989). Delay of gratification in children. Science, 244(4907), 933-938.

Mueller, C.M. & Dweck, C.S. (1998). Praise for intelligence can undermine children's motivation and performance. Journal of Personality and Social Psychology, 75, 33-52.

National Scientific Council on the Developing Child (2004). *Children's emotional development is built into the architecture of their brains.* Working Paper No. 2.

National Scientific Council on the Developing Child (2010). *Early experiences can alter gene expression and affect long-term development.* Working Paper No. 10.

National Scientific Council on the Developing Child (2005). *Excessive stress disrupts the architecture of the developing brain.* Working Paper No. 3.

National Scientific Council on the Developing Child. (2007). *The Science of Early Childhood Development: Closing the Gap Between What We Know and What We Do.* http://developingchild.harvard.edu/library/reports_

and_working_papers/science_of_early_childhood_ development/

National Scientific Council on the Developing Child. (2008). *The timing and quality of early experiences combine to shape brain architecture.* Working Paper No.5.

National Scientific Council on the Developing Child. (2004). *Young children develop in an environment of relationships.* Working Paper No.1.

National Scientific Council on the Developing Child. (2010). *Persistent fear and anxiety can affect young children's learning and development.* Working Paper No. 9. http://developingchild.harvard.edu/library/ reports_and_working_papers/working_papers/wp9/

*National Television Violence Study* (1996). Executive summary, volume 1. Studio City, CA: Mediascope.

Nelson, C. (2004). Brain development during puberty and adolescence: Comments on part II. *Annals of the New York Academy of Sciences, 1021*(1). pp. 105-109.

Nelson, C., Thomas, K., & DeHaan, M. (2006). Neural bases of cognitive development. In D. Kuhn & R.S. Siegler (Eds.), *Handbook of child psychology*, 6th edition, volume 2, chapter 16. Hoboken, N.J.: John Wiley & Sons. pp. 3-19 and 35-39.

Nelson, C., Furtado, E., Fox, A., & Zeanah, C. (2009). The deprived human brain. *American Scientist*, 97, 222-229. http://www.americanscientist.org/issues/ id.6380,y.2009,no.3,content.true,page.4,css.print/ issue.aspx

Newport, C. (2010). How to be a high school superstar: A revolutionary plan to get into college by standing out (without burning out). New York: Random House. pp. 1-242.

NICHD Early Child Care Research Network (1996). Characteristics of infant child care: Factors contributing to positive caregiving. Early Childhood Research Quarterly, 11. pp. 296-306.

NICHD Early Child Care Research Network (2000). Characteristics and quality of child care for toddlers and preschoolers. Applied Developmental Science, 4(3). pp. 116-125.

Piaget, J. (1952[1936]). The origins of intelligence in children. International University Press.

Piaget, J. & Szeminska, A. (1941). The child's conception of number. Selected pages reprinted in Gruber, H.E.& Voneche, J.J. (1977). *The essential Piaget*. New Jersey: Jason Aronson Inc. pp. 298-311.

Posner, M.I., Sheese, B.E., Odludas, Y., Tang, Y.Y. (2006). Analyzing and shaping human attentional networks. Neural Networks, 19, 1422-1429.

Raz, A. & Buhle, J. (2006). Typologies of attentional networks. Nature Reviews, 7, 367-379.

Repitti R., Taylor S., Seeman T. (2002). Risky families: Family social environments and the mental and physical health of offspring. *Psychological Bulletin,* 128. pp. 330-366. http://repettilab.psych.ucla. edu/repetti%20taylor%20seeman%202002.pdf

Rideout, V., Roberts, D., and Foehr, U. (2005). *Generation M: Media in the lives of 8-18 year-olds.* Executive summary. Menlo Park, CA: Henry J. Kaiser Family Foundation.

Rideout, V., Roberts, D., and Foehr, U. (2010). *Generation M2: Media in the lives of 8-18 year-olds.* Executive summary. Menlo Park, CA: Henry J. Kaiser Family Foundation.

Rideout, V., and Hamel, E. (2006). *The media family: Electronic media in the lives of infants, toddlers, preschoolers, and their parents.* Menlo Park, CA: Henry J. Kaiser Family Foundation.

Rose, D. and Dalton, B. (2009). Learning to read in the digital age. *Mind, Brain, and Education*, 3(2). pp. 74-83.

Rose, D. and Gavel, J. (2012). Curricular opportunities in the digital age. Students at the center series, Boston: Jobs for the future. Retrieved online from www. studentsatthecenter.org/papers/curricular-opportunities- digital-age.

Rose, D. and Meyer, A. (2002). Teaching every student in the digital age: Universal design for learning. Alexandria, VA: Association for Supervision and Curriculum Development. pp. 1-174.

Rose, L. T. & Fischer, K. W. (2009). Dynamic systems theory. In R.A. Shweder (Ed.), *Chicago Companion to the Child.* Chicago: University of Chicago Press. pp. 1-6.

Rose, L.T., Rouhani, P., & Fischer, K.W. (2013). The science of the individual. Mind, Brain, and Education, 7, 3, 152-158.

Sadler, W. (2009). *Langman's medical embryology, eleventh edition: North American edition.* Philadelphia, PA: Lippincott Williams & Wilkins (pp. 36-54, 293-300).

Sapolsky, R., Romero, L., & Munck, A. (2000). How do glucocorticoids influence stress responses? Integrating permissive, suppressive, stimulatory and preparative actions. *Endocrine Reviews*, 21(1), pp. 55-89.

Schmidt, M., and Anderson, D. (2006). The impact of television on cognitive development and educational achievement. In N. Pecora, J. P. Murray, and E. A. Wartella, (Eds.). *Children and television: Fifty years of research.* Mahwah, NJ: Lawrence Erlbaum Associates.

Sebastian, C., Viding, E., Williams, K.D., & Blakemore, S.J. (2010). Social brain development and the affective consequences of ostracism in adolescence. Brain and Cognition, 72, 134-145.

Shonkoff, J., Boyce, W.T., & McEwen, B.S. (2009). Neuroscience, molecular biology, and the childhood roots of health disparities: Building a new framework for health promotion and disease prevention. *Journal of the American Medical Association, 301*, 2252-2259.

Shonkoff, J. (2000). Science, policy, and practice: Three cultures in search of a shared mission. *Child Development*, 71. pp. 181-187.

Siegler, R. (2003). Implications of cognitive science research for mathematics education. In J. Kilpatrick, W.B. Martin, & D.E. Schifter (Eds.), *A research companion to principles and standards for school mathematics*. Reston, VA: National Council of Teachers of Mathematics. pp. 219-233.

Sikstrom, S. & Soderlund, G. (2007). Stimulus-dependent dopamine release in attention deficit hyperactivity disorder. Psychological Review, 114(4), 1047-1075.

Singer, D. and Singer, J. (Eds.). (2001). *Handbook of children and the media*. Thousand Oaks, CA: Sage Publications.

Smith, S., Smith, S., Pieper, K., Yoo, K., Ferris, A., Downs, E and Bowden, B. (2006). Altruism on american television: Examining the amount of, and context surrounding, acts of helping and sharing. *Journal of Communication, 56*, pp. 707-727.

Sparrow, B., Liu, J., Wgner, D. M. (2011). Google Effects on Memory: Cognitive Consequences of Having Information at Our Fingertips. Science, 333, 776-778. (DOI: 10.1126/science.1207745).

Spearman, C. (1904). General intelligence, objectively determined and measured. The American Journal of Psychology, 15, 2, 201-292.

Spitzer, M. (2000). The mind within a net. Cambridge, MA: MIT Press.

Steele, C. (1997). A threat in the air: How stereotypes shape intellectual identity and performance. *American Psychologist, 52*(6), pp. 613-629.

Stein, Z., Dawson, T. & Fischer, K. (2010). Redesigning testing: Operationalizing the new science of learning. In Khine &Saleh (Eds.). *The new science of learning: Computers, cognition and collaboration education*. Springer Press.

Steinberg, L. (2008). A social neuroscience perspective on adolescent risk-taking. Developmental Review, 28, 78-106.

Steinberg, L. (2009). Should the science of adolescent brain development inform public policy? American Psychologist, November Issue, 739-750.

Sternberg, R. (1996). Successful intelligence: How practical and creative intelligence determine success in life. New York: Simon and Schuster.

Sternberg, R. (1997). Thinking Styles. Cambridge: University Press.

Sylvan, L. and Christodoulou, J. (2010). Understanding the role of neuroscience in brain-based products: A guide for educators and consumers. *Mind, Brain, and Education*, 4(1). pp. 1-7.

Sylwester, R. (2007). The adolescent brain reaching for automomy. Thousand Oaks, CA: Corwin Press. pp.1-139.

Szucs, D. & Goswami, U., (2007). Educational neuroscience: Defining a new discipline for the study of mental representations. *Mind, Brain, and Education, 1*(3), pp. 114-127.

Thompson, R. and Nelson, C. (2001). Developmental science and the media. American Psychologist, 56(1). pp. 5-15.

Thompson, R. & Lagattuta, K. (2006). Feeling and understanding: Early emotional development. In K. McCartney & D. Phillips (Eds.), The Blackwell Handbook of Early Childhood Development. Oxford, UK: Blackwell. pp. 317-337.

Van Praag, H., Kempermann, G. & Gage, F.H. (2000). Neural consequences of environmental enrichment. Nature Reviews Neuroscience, 1, 191-198.

Vygotsky, L. (1978). Mind and society: The development of higher psychological processes. Cambridge, MA: MIT Press.

Vygotsky, L. (1986). Thought and language. Cambridge, MA: MIT Press. pp. 190-208.

Waldfogel, J. (1999).The impact of the family and medical leave act. Journal of Policy Analysis and Management, 18(2). pp. 281-302.

Weinberger, D., Elvevag, B. & Giedd, J. (2005). The adolescent brain: A work in progress. The National Campaign to Prevent Teen Pregnancy. TEENPREGNANCY.org

Weiss, C.H. (1995). Nothing as practical as good theory: Exploring theory-based evaluation for comprehensive community initiatives for children and families. In J.P. Connell, A.C. Kubisch, L.B. Schorr, & C.H. Weiss (Eds.), *New approaches to evaluating community initiatives: Concepts, methods and contexts* (pp. 65-92). Washington , DC: The Aspen Institute. http://aspe.hhs.gov/pic/reports/aspe/5895.pdf#page=83

Weaver, I., Diorio, J., Seckl, J., Szyf, M., & Meaney, M. (2004). Early environmental regulation of hippocampal glucocorticoid receptor gene expression: Characterization of intracellular mediators and potential genomic target sites. Annals of the New York Academy of Sciences, 1024. pp. 182-212.

Worden, J., Hinton, C. & Fischer, K. (2011). What does the brain have to do with learning? *Phi Delta Kappan*, 92(8). pp. 8-11.

Yoshikawa, H., & Hsueh, J. (2001). Child development and public policy: Toward a dynamic systems perspective. *Child Development, 72*, 1887-1903.

Zito, J., Safer, D., dosReis, S., Gardner, J., Boles, M., & Lynch, F. (2000).Trends in the prescribing of psychotropic medications to preschoolers. Journal of the American Medical Association, 283(8). pp. 1025-1030.

---

**ADOLESCENT SLEEP PATTERNS, RESEARCH STUDIES**

Acebo, C. and Carskadon, M. (2002). Influence of irregular sleep/wake patterns on waking behavior. In *Adolescent Sleep Patterns: Biological, Social, and Psychological Influences*, M. Carskadon (Ed.), Cambridge: University Press, pp. 220-235.

Carskadon, M.A. (Editor). (2002). *Adolescent Sleep Patterns: Biological, Social, and Psychological Influences.* Cambridge: University Press.

Carskadon, M. (2002). Factors influencing sleep patterns of adolescents. In *Adolescent Sleep Patterns: Biological, Social, and Psychological Influences*, M.A. Carskadon (Ed.), Cambridge: University Press. pp. 4-26.

Carskadon, M.A. (2008). Maturation of processes regulating sleep in adolescents. In Marcus, C., Carroll, J., Donnelly, D., and Loughlin, G. (Eds.). *Sleep in Children, Second Edition.* Informa Healthcare USA, New York, pp 95-114.

Carskadon, M., Harvey, K., Duke, P., Anders, T., Litt, I., & Dement, W. (1980). Pubertal changes in daytime sleepiness. *Sleep* 2: pp. 453-460.

Carskadon, M., Acebo, C., & Jenni, O. (2004). Regulation of adolescent sleep: Implications for behavior. *Ann. N.Y. Acad. Sci.* 1021: pp. 276-291.

Carskadon, M. (2002). Risks of driving while sleepy in adolescents and young adults. In *Adolescent Sleep Patterns: Biological, Social, and Psychological Influences*, M. Carskadon (Ed.), Cambridge: University Press. pp. 148-158.

Carskadon, M. (2009). Sleep, adolescence, and learning. *Frontiers Neuroscience, 3(3).* pp. 470-471.

Carskadon, M. (2005) Sleep and circadian rhythms in children and adolescents: Implications for athletic performance of young people. *Clin Sports Med* 24: pp. 319-328.

Carskadon, M. and Tarokh, L. (2009). Sleep in child and adolescent development. In Klockars, M. and Porkka-Heiskanen, T. (Eds.) *The Many Aspects of Sleep.* Acta Gyllenbergiana VIII. Helsinki: The Signe and Ane Gyllenberg Foundation, pp 89-100.

Carskadon, M. (1999). When worlds collide: Adolescent need for sleep versus societal demands. *Phi Delta Kappan.* **80(5).** pp. 348-349.

Dahl, R. (2004a). Adolescent development and the regulation of behavior and emotion: Introduction to part VIII. *Annals of the New York Academy of Sciences, 1021(1).* pp. 294-295.

Dahl, R. (2008). Biological, developmental, and neurobehavioral factors related to adolescent driving risks. American Journal of Preventative Medicine, 35(3).

Dahl, R. (2004b). Adolescent brain development: A period of vulnerabilities and opportunities. Keynote address. *Annals of the New York Academy of Sciences, 1021(1).* pp. 1-22.

Dahl, R., and Spear, L. (2004). *Adolescent brain development: Vulnerabilities and opportunities.* New York: New York Academy of Sciences.

Dahl, R. and Carskadon, M. (1995). Sleep and its disorders in adolescence. In *Principles and Practice of Sleep Medicine in the Child,* R.Ferber and M. Kryger (Eds.), W.B. Saunders, Philadelphia. pp. 19-27.

Dement, W. and Carskadon, M. (1982) Current perspectives on daytime sleepiness: The issues. *Sleep* 5: pp. S56-S66.

Dement, W. and Carskadon, M. (1983). Daytime drowsiness: When it indicates a clinically significant problem. *Consultant* 23. pp. 182-199.

Dement, W. and Vaughan, C. (1999). The promise of sleep: A pioneer in sleep medicine explores the vital connection between health,happiness, and a good night's sleep. New York: Dell.

Giedd J. (2005). *Root causes of teen driving accidents, II,* The Allstate Foundation State of Teen Driving Report. http://media.allstate.com/releases/4206-new-research-on-teen.

Giedd J., Blumenthal, J., Jeffries, N., Castellanos, F., Liu H., Zijdenbos, A., et al. (1999). Brain development during childhood and adolescence: A longitudinal MRI study. *Nature Neuroscience, 2.* pp. 861-863.

Giedd, J. (2004). Structural magnetic resonance imaging of the adolescent brain. *Annals of the New York Academy of Sciences, 1021(1).* pp. 77-85.

Jenni, O. and Carskadon, M. (Guest Eds.). (2007). *Sleep Medicine Clinics: Sleep in Children and Adolescents.* Philadelphia. W.B. Saunders (Elsevier), Philadelphia.

Kirby, M., Maggi, S., & D'Angiulli, A. (2011). School start times and the sleep-wake cycle of adolescents: A review and critical evaluation of available evidence. Educational Researcher, 40(2), 56-61.

Society for Neuroscience. (2006). Brain facts: A primer on the brain and nervous system. *Sleep. Stress.* Canada. pp. 4-60.

# NOTES

# NOTES

# NOTES

# NOTES

# NOTES

# NOTES

# NOTES

# NOTES

# NOTES